Taste of H

CAST IRON

100 ESSENTIAL SKILLET RECIPES

TASTE OF HOME BOOKS • RDA ENTHUSIAST BRANDS, LLC • MILWAUKEE, WI

Taste*of*Home

© 2018 RDA Enthusiast Brands, LLC
1610 N. 2nd St., Suite 102, Milwaukee WI 53212

Visit us at **tasteofhome.com** for other
Taste of Home books and products.

International Standard Book Number:
978-1-61765-740-5

Library of Congress Control Number:
2018935109

Cover Photographer: Mark Derse
Set Stylist: Stephanie Marchese
Food Stylist: Kathryn Conrad

Pictured on front cover:
Cast-Iron Peach Crostata, p. 76

Pictured on spine:
Focaccia Barese, p. 38

Pictured on title page:
Butternut Squash Rolls, p.137

Pictured on this page:
Cheesy Pizza Rolls, p.104

**Pictured on back cover
(from left):**
Waffle Fry Nachos, p. 9;
Skillet Chicken Fajitas, p. 103

Printed in China.
1 3 5 7 9 10 8 6 4 2

GET SOCIAL WITH US

To find a recipe tasteofhome.com
To submit a recipe tasteofhome.com/submit
To find out about other *Taste of Home* products shoptasteofhome.com

 LIKE US
facebook.com/tasteofhome

TWEET US
twitter.com/tasteofhome

 FOLLOW US
@tasteofhome

PIN US
pinterest.com/taste_of_home

TABLE OF CONTENTS

A Crash Course in **CAST IRON**

Durable and versatile, the cast-iron skillet is a true kitchen workhorse that will last a lifetime and cook almost anything—from breakfast to one-dish dinners to delicious desserts. Whether your skillet is new, a family heirloom or a flea market find, take some time to learn how to treat it right, then get started with the recipes in this book!

HOW TO SEASON A CAST-IRON SKILLET

Clean. Scrub with hot water and a stiff brush to remove any rust.

Oil. Drop a tablespoon of vegetable oil on the pan; spread it around with a paper towel. Oil the entire outside of the skillet, including the handle. Wipe off excess oil with a folded paper towel. The skillet should be just lightly greased.

Heat. Set the oven to 350°; put a piece of foil on the bottom rack. Place the skillet, face down, on the upper rack for about an hour, letting it heat up with the oven. Turn the oven off; leave the pan inside until it's cool. The oil bakes into the pores of the pan, creating a nonstick finish.

Repeat. Do it all over again for an almost glassy surface of seasoning.

HOW TO SAVE A RUSTY SKILLET

Scour. Get the pan wet, add a little dish soap, then scrub with a piece of steel wool or a tough scrubber. Scrub in small circles, focusing on the most rusted parts first. Scrub until you see the original black iron emerge, then rinse.

Scrub with a sponge. To make sure the skillet is clean, scrub again—this time with a soapy sponge. Buff off any residue or rusty bits that remain.

Dry. Use a clean dishrag to dry the skillet. Don't use a rag you're fond of; the iron can leave dark stains. To dry it completely, place the skillet on the stove and turn on the heat for a couple of minutes.

For small jobs: For a newer pan that has small amounts of rust but doesn't need a complete scouring and cleaning, simply dampen a paper towel with oil and use it to wipe away the rust.

HOW TO CARE FOR CAST IRON

- **DO** clean immediately after use (*after* the pan cools).

- **DO** wait until the pan is cool to the touch before washing it in the sink. Submerging hot cast iron in cold water can cause it to crack.

- **DO** use hot water and soap. It's a common misconception that soap will strip the seasoning from cast iron, so go ahead and suds up.

- **DON'T** let it soak too long. Cast iron + extended exposure to water = rust.

CAMPFIRE ICON

Throughout this book, you'll see the Campfire Ready icon, which identifies recipes that can be made outdoors. These simple, classic recipes don't require oven baking, complicated prep work or changing the temperature of the heat source. They're ideal for your next campfire cookout!

COMMON STOVETOP COOKING TECHNIQUES

SEARING: Heat oil in a large cast-iron or other ovenproof skillet over medium-high heat until it begins to smoke. Cook the meat, poultry or fish until a deeply colored crust has formed. Reduce the heat if the food browns too quickly. Pat the food dry before cooking and don't overcrowd the pan.

FRYING: Pour a half-inch of oil into a skillet. Heat over medium-high until hot. When the oil shimmers (gives off visible waves of heat), it's ready. Never leave the pan unattended, and don't overheat the oil or it will smoke. Pat food dry before frying and, if desired, dip in batter or coat with crumbs. Don't overcrowd the pan, as this will cause the food to steam rather than fry. Fry, uncovered, until food is golden brown and cooked through.

SAUTEING: Pour a small amount of oil into a skillet. Heat over medium-high until hot. For best results, the food should be cut into uniformly sized pieces and patted dry before cooking. Don't overcrowd the pan. Stir frequently.

171

43

TYPES OF
HEAVY METAL

The two most common types of cast iron are traditional bare cast iron and enameled cast iron. They behave similarly, but there are some notable differences. Here's the rundown to help you rock your cast-iron cooking.

TRADITIONAL CAST IRON
PROS
- Inexpensive
- Can be used over an open flame, such as a grill or campfire
- Practically indestructible and will last a lifetime (maybe longer!) if properly seasoned and cared for
- Food not likely to stick if the iron is properly seasoned

CONS
- Prone to rust; needs to be seasoned every once in a while
- Not practical for all foods; tomatoes and other acidic ingredients will cause seasoning to wear off
- May retain flavors of foods, such as fried fish, after using

ENAMELED CAST IRON

PROS

- Available in a variety of attractive colors
- Can cook acidic ingredients without harming surface
- Does not retain flavors of foods after using

CONS

- Can be expensive
- Not as durable as traditional cast iron; enamel coating can chip if mishandled
- Food more likely to stick than on traditional cast iron
- Takes a little longer to heat up than traditional cast iron

OTHER OVENPROOF OPTIONS

Many of the recipes in this book call for ovenproof skillets. As an alternative to cast iron, you can also use skillets made of:

- Copper
- Aluminum
- Anodized Aluminum
- Stainless Steel

DO NOT use nonstick (Teflon) skillets in the oven, or any cookware that has plastic elements.

SNACKS &
STARTERS

WAFFLE FRY NACHOS

My husband and two grown sons really enjoy this cheesy appetizer. They can devour a platter in no time. The snack is also a fun change-of-pace to serve when friends are over. In addition to a great party food, the nachos make a fun side dish, too!
—**DEBRA MORGAN** IDAHO FALLS, ID

START TO FINISH: 25 MIN.
MAKES: 8 SERVINGS

- 1 **package (22 ounces) frozen waffle fries**
- 10 **bacon strips, cooked and crumbled**
- 3 **green onions, sliced**
- 1 **can (6 ounces) sliced ripe olives, drained**
- 2 **medium tomatoes, seeded and chopped**
- ⅔ **cup salsa**
- 1½ **cups shredded cheddar cheese**
- 1½ **cups shredded Monterey Jack cheese**
  Sour cream

Bake fries according to the package directions. Transfer them to a 10-in. ovenproof skillet. Top with the bacon, onions, olives, tomatoes, salsa and cheeses. Return to oven for 5 minutes or until cheese is melted. Serve with sour cream.

CHICKEN CORN FRITTERS

I have always loved corn fritters, but couldn't find a perfect recipe. I came up with this variation and was thrilled when my husband and our three young boys gave it rave reviews. The chicken and zesty chili sauce make the fritters a wonderful treat.

—MARIE GREENE SCOTTSBLUFF, NE

PREP: 20 MIN. • **COOK:** 15 MIN.
MAKES: 1 DOZEN

- 1 can (15¼ ounces) whole kernel corn, drained
- 1 cup finely chopped cooked chicken
- 1 large egg, lightly beaten
- ½ cup milk
- 2 tablespoons butter, melted
- ½ teaspoon salt
- ⅛ teaspoon pepper
- 1¾ cups all-purpose flour
- 1 teaspoon baking powder
  Oil for deep-fat frying

GREEN CHILI SAUCE

- ⅓ cup butter, cubed
- ¼ cup all-purpose flour
- ¼ teaspoon salt
- ⅛ teaspoon pepper
- ⅛ teaspoon garlic powder
- ⅛ teaspoon ground cumin
- 1 can (4 ounces) chopped green chilies
- 1 cup milk
  Shredded cheddar cheese, optional

1. Place corn in a large bowl; lightly crush with a potato masher. Stir in the chicken, egg, milk, butter, salt and pepper. Combine flour and baking powder; stir into the corn mixture just until combined.

2. In a skillet or deep-fat fryer, heat 2 in. of oil to 375°. Drop batter by ¼ cupfuls into oil. Fry for 3 minutes on each side or until golden brown. Drain on paper towels; keep warm.

3. In a large saucepan, melt butter over medium-low heat. Stir in flour and seasonings until smooth. Add chilies. Gradually stir in milk. Bring to a boil; cook and stir for 2 minutes or until thickened. Serve with the corn fritters; sprinkle with cheese if desired.

HELPFUL HINT

Try not to reuse cooking oil since quality and flavor are compromised once oil is heated. Also, tiny food particles may be released, causing off-flavors in the foods being cooked.

BERRY WHIRLIGIG

PREP: 25 MIN. • **BAKE:** 25 MIN.
MAKES: 9 SERVINGS

- ½ cup sugar
- 2 tablespoons cornstarch
- ½ teaspoon salt
- ¼ teaspoon ground cinnamon
- 1 cup water
- 3 cups fresh or frozen blackberries or a mixture of berries

WHIRLIGIGS

- 1 cup all-purpose flour
- 2 teaspoons baking powder
- ½ teaspoon salt
- 2 tablespoons shortening
- 1 large egg, lightly beaten
- 2 tablespoons milk
- ¼ cup butter, softened
- ½ cup sugar
- 1 teaspoon grated lemon peel
- ¼ teaspoon ground cinnamon

1. In a large saucepan, combine the sugar, cornstarch, salt and cinnamon. Stir in the water until smooth. Cook until mixture boils and thickens. Stir in berries; cook over low heat for 5 minutes.

2. Pour into a greased 9- or 10-in. cast-iron skillet or 8-in. square baking pan; set aside. In a large bowl, combine the flour, baking powder and salt. Cut in shortening until coarse crumbs form.

3. In a small bowl, mix the egg and milk. Add to flour mixture; stir until the mixture forms a soft ball. Knead several minutes. Roll into a 12x8-in. rectangle. Spread with the butter. Combine sugar, peel and cinnamon; sprinkle over dough.

4. Starting at a long end, roll up; seal edges. Cut into 9 slices. Place slices over berry mixture. Bake at 400° for 22-25 minutes or until golden brown.

We love to go out and pick our own blackberries. Whatever we don't eat fresh we freeze, to enjoy whenever we start dreaming of this irresistible treat.

—PEARL STANFORD MEDFORD, OR

MANDARIN CHICKEN BITES

Instead of big holiday meals, our family enjoys nibbling on an all-day appetizer buffets. Each time, we present tempting new dishes alongside our favorites. This is one of those tried-and-true bites that's a must for us.

—SUSANNAH YINGER CANAL WINCHESTER, OH

START TO FINISH: 30 MIN.
MAKES: 12-15 SERVINGS

- 1 **cup all-purpose flour**
- ½ **teaspoon salt**
- ¼ **teaspoon pepper**
- 1 **pound boneless skinless chicken breasts, cut into 2-inch cubes**
- 2 **tablespoons butter**
- 1 **can (11 ounces) mandarin oranges, drained**
- ⅔ **cup orange marmalade**
- ½ **teaspoon dried tarragon**

1. In a large resealable plastic bag, combine the flour, salt and pepper. Add chicken, a few pieces at a time, and shake to coat.

2. In a skillet, brown chicken in butter until no longer pink. In a small saucepan, combine the oranges, marmalade and tarragon; bring to a boil. Pour over chicken; stir gently to coat. Serve warm with toothpicks.

CHEESY SKILLET PIZZA DIP

Get ready to add a new favorite to your appetizer lineup. Perfect for just about any occasion, this hearty snack has the dippers baked right in.

—*TASTE OF HOME* **TEST KITCHEN**

PREP: 25 MIN. + RISING • **BAKE:** 25 MIN.
MAKES: 18 SERVINGS

- 6 **tablespoons butter**
- 1 **teaspoon garlic powder, divided**
- ¼ **teaspoon crushed red pepper flakes**
- 1 **package (16 ounces) frozen bread dough dinner rolls, thawed**
- 1 **package (8 ounces) cream cheese, softened**
- 1½ **cups shredded part-skim mozzarella cheese, divided**
- 1 **cup mayonnaise**
- 1 **teaspoon Italian seasoning**
- ½ **cup pizza sauce**
- ¼ **cup (¾ ounce) sliced pepperoni**
- 2 **tablespoons shredded Parmesan cheese**
- 2 **tablespoons minced fresh basil**

1. Microwave butter, ½ teaspoon garlic powder and red pepper flakes, covered, until butter is melted. Cut each roll into thirds; roll each piece into a ball. Dip dough balls in butter mixture; place along the outer edge of a 10-in. cast-iron skillet, leaving the center open. Gently stack the remaining balls on top of bottom layer, leaving some space between them. Cover and let rise till balls are almost doubled, about 30 minutes.

2. Preheat oven to 400°. Bake until dough balls are set and beginning to brown, 15-18 minutes.

3. Meanwhile, combine the cream cheese, 1 cup mozzarella cheese, mayonnaise, Italian seasoning and remaining garlic powder; spoon into center of skillet. Layer with ¼ cup mozzarella and pizza sauce. Top with the remaining mozzarella and pepperoni. Brush rolls with some of remaining butter mixture; sprinkle with Parmesan.

4. Bake until dip is heated through and rolls are golden brown, about 10 minutes, covering loosely with foil as needed to prevent the rolls from becoming too dark. Sprinkle with the basil.

BACON CHEESEBURGER BALLS

When I serve these, guests sometimes think they're in for plain meatballs. Boy, are they surprised when they discover the flavorful filling inside. What a party pleaser!

—CATHY LENDVOY BOHARM, SK

PREP: 25 MIN. • **COOK:** 10 MIN. • **MAKES:** 3 DOZEN

- 1 **large egg**
- 1 **envelope onion soup mix**
- 1 **pound ground beef**
- 2 **tablespoons all-purpose flour**
- 2 **tablespoons 2% milk**
- 1 **cup shredded cheddar cheese**
- 4 **bacon strips, cooked and crumbled**

COATING

- 2 **large eggs**
- 1 **cup crushed saltines (about 30 crackers)**
- 5 **tablespoons canola oil**

1. In a large bowl, combine egg and soup mix. Crumble beef over mixture and mix well. Divide into 36 portions; set aside. In another large bowl, combine the flour and milk until smooth. Add cheese and bacon; mix well.

2. Shape the cheese mixture into 36 balls. Shape one beef portion around each cheese ball. In a shallow bowl, beat eggs. Place cracker crumbs in another bowl. Dip meatballs into egg, then coat with crumbs.

3. In a large skillet, cook meatballs over medium heat in oil for 10-12 minutes or until the meat is no longer pink and coating is golden brown.

HOT SAUSAGE & BEAN DIP

This is a spin-off of a Mexican dip that I once had. The original was wicked good, but I was passing through an I'm-so-over-Mexican-dip phase and decided to switch it up. If you take this one to a party, you can be sure that no one else will bring anything like it!

—MANDY RIVERS LEXINGTON, SC

PREP: 25 MIN. • **BAKE:** 20 MIN.
MAKES: 16 SERVINGS

- 1 pound bulk hot Italian sausage
- 1 medium onion, finely chopped
- 4 garlic cloves, minced
- ½ cup dry white wine or chicken broth
- ½ teaspoon dried oregano
- ¼ teaspoon salt
- ¼ teaspoon dried thyme
- 1 package (8 ounces) cream cheese, softened
- 1 package (6 ounces) fresh baby spinach, coarsely chopped
- 1 can (15 ounces) cannellini beans, rinsed and drained
- 1 cup chopped seeded tomatoes
- 1 cup shredded part-skim mozzarella cheese
- ½ cup shredded Parmesan cheese
   Assorted crackers or toasted French bread baguette slices

1. Preheat oven to 375°. In a large skillet, cook the sausage, onion and garlic over medium heat until the sausage is no longer pink, breaking up sausage into crumbles; drain. Stir in the wine, oregano, salt and thyme. Bring to a boil; cook until liquid is almost evaporated.

2. Add cream cheese; stir until melted. Stir in spinach, beans and tomatoes; cook and stir until the spinach is wilted. Transfer to a greased 8-in. square or if using an oven-proof skillet, leave in skillet. Sprinkle with cheeses.

3. Bake until bubbly, for 20-25 minutes. Serve with crackers.

HELPFUL HINT

Leftover dip is sensational for lunch the next day. Simply wrap it in a spinach- or tomato-flavored tortilla with some leafy greens. Add a cup of soup for a no-fuss dinner!

CHILI CHICKEN STRIPS

Here, instead of ordinary bread crumbs, seasoned crushed corn chips coat these slightly crunchy chicken fingers. If your family likes food with some zip, use the full 1½ teaspoons of chili powder.

—*TASTE OF HOME* TEST KITCHEN

START TO FINISH: 25 MIN.
MAKES: 6 SERVINGS

- ¾ cup crushed corn chips
- 2 tablespoons dry bread crumbs
- 1 tablespoon all-purpose flour
- 1 to 1½ teaspoons chili powder
- ½ teaspoon seasoned salt
- ½ teaspoon poultry seasoning
- ¼ teaspoon pepper
- ¼ teaspoon paprika
- 1 large egg
- 1½ pounds boneless skinless chicken breasts, cut into ½-inch strips
- 4 tablespoons butter, divided

1. In a shallow bowl, combine the first eight ingredients. In another shallow bowl, beat egg. Dip chicken in egg, then roll in corn-chip mixture.

2. In a large skillet, cook half of the chicken in 2 tablespoons butter for 8-10 minutes or until the meat is no longer pink. Repeat with remaining chicken and butter.

CAMPFIRE READY

MEXICAN SALSA

PREP: 40 MIN. • **MAKES:** 3½ CUPS

- 3 **jalapeno peppers**
- 1 **medium onion, quartered**
- 1 **garlic clove, halved**
- 2 **cans (one 28 ounces, one 14½ ounces) whole tomatoes, drained**
- 4 **fresh cilantro sprigs**
- ½ **teaspoon salt**
  Tortilla chips

1. Heat a small ungreased cast-iron skillet over high heat. With a small sharp knife, pierce the jalapenos; add to hot skillet. Cook for 15-20 minutes or until the peppers are blistered and blackened, turning occasionally.

2. Immediately place the jalapenos in a small bowl; cover and let stand for 20 minutes. Peel off and discard charred skins. Remove stems and seeds.

3. Place onion and garlic in a food processor; cover and pulse four times. Add the tomatoes, cilantro, salt and jalapenos. Cover and process until desired consistency. Chill until serving. Serve with chips.

NOTE *Wear disposable gloves when cutting hot peppers; the oils can burn skin. Avoid touching your face.*

This zippy salsa is excellent any time of year, but I love to make it with fresh tomatoes and peppers from my garden. I even have a special pan for roasting the peppers! We like it with blue tortilla chips.

—ROGER STENMAN BATAVIA, IL

JALAPENO CRAB DIP

Set this appetizer dip out for a football game, birthday party or even for an elegant holiday get-together. It is so worth the effort to prepare.
—**ERIN CONNER** RIVERSIDE, CA

PREP: 30 MIN. • **BAKE:** 30 MIN.
MAKES: 24 SERVINGS

- 2 **tablespoons butter, divided**
- 1½ **cups frozen corn**
- ½ **teaspoon salt**
- ½ **teaspoon pepper**
- 1 **large onion, chopped**
- 1 **small sweet red pepper, chopped**
- 2 **green onions, chopped**
- 1 **to 2 tablespoons chopped seeded jalapeno pepper**
- 1 **garlic clove, minced**
- 2 **cans (6 ounces each) lump crabmeat, drained**
- 1½ **cups shredded pepper jack cheese**
- 1½ **cups shredded cheddar cheese**
- 1 **cup mayonnaise**
- ¼ **cup chopped pickled jalapeno slices**
- 1 **teaspoon Louisiana-style hot sauce**
- 1 **teaspoon Worcestershire sauce**
- ⅔ **cup grated Parmesan cheese**
  Tortilla chips

1. Preheat oven to 350°. In a large cast-iron or other ovenproof skillet, heat 1 tablespoon of butter over medium-high heat. Add corn, salt and pepper; cook and stir until corn is golden brown. Remove from pan.

2. In same skillet, heat remaining butter over medium-high heat. Add onion and red pepper; cook and stir until onion is tender. Add the green onions, fresh jalapeno and garlic; cook 1-2 minutes longer. Remove from heat.

3. In a large bowl, combine crab, pepper jack cheese, cheddar cheese, mayonnaise, pickled jalapenos, hot sauce and Worcestershire sauce; stir in the corn and onion mixture. Transfer to same skillet or a greased 8-in. square baking dish; sprinkle with Parmesan cheese.

4. Bake, uncovered, 30-35 minutes or until edges are golden brown. Serve with chips.

NOTE *Wear disposable gloves when cutting hot peppers; the oils can burn skin. Avoid touching your face.*

MARINATED SHRIMP

My husband's aunt shared this recipe with me more than 20 years ago. Not only is it a special-occasion tradition in my home, but in the homes of our grown children as well.

—DELORES HILL HELENA, MT

PREP: 5 MIN. + MARINATING • **BAKE:** 10 MIN.
MAKES: 4-6 SERVINGS

- 2 **pounds uncooked jumbo shrimp, peeled and deveined**
- 1 **cup olive oil**
- 2 **garlic cloves, minced**
- 4 **teaspoons dried rosemary, crushed**
- 2 **teaspoons dried oregano**
- 2 **bay leaves**
- 1 **cup dry white wine or chicken broth**
- ¾ **teaspoon salt**
- ⅛ **teaspoon pepper**

1. In a large bowl, combine shrimp, oil, garlic, rosemary, oregano and bay leaves. Cover it and refrigerate for 2-4 hours.

2. Pour shrimp and marinade into a large deep skillet. Add wine or broth, salt and pepper. Cover and cook over medium-low heat for 10-15 minutes or until shrimp turn pink, stirring occasionally. Discard bay leaves. Transfer with a slotted spoon to a serving dish.

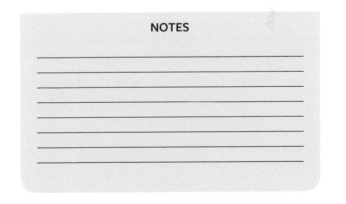

NOTES

SAUSAGE DIP

START TO FINISH: 30 MIN.
MAKES: 6 CUPS

- 1½ **pounds bulk pork sausage**
- 2½ **cups chopped fresh mushrooms**
- 2 **medium green peppers, chopped**
- 1 **large tomato, seeded and chopped**
- 1 **medium red onion, chopped**
- 1½ **teaspoons salt**
- 1 **teaspoon pepper**
- 1 **teaspoon garlic powder**
- ½ **teaspoon onion powder**
- 2 **packages (8 ounces each) cream cheese, cubed**
- 1 **cup (8 ounces) sour cream**
  Tortilla chips

In a large skillet over medium heat, cook the sausage until no longer pink; drain. Add the next eight ingredients; cook until the vegetables are tender. Reduce heat to low; add cream cheese and sour cream. Cook and stir until cheese is melted and well blended (do not boil). Serve warm with tortilla chips.

This warm sausage dip is a family-favorite snack on cool fall days. The men in your family will especially love this country-style appetizer.

—SUSIE WINGERT PANAMA, IA

CHINESE SCALLION PANCAKES

Unlike true pancakes, Cong You Bing (or Chinese scallion pancakes) are made from a dough instead of a batter. The tasty appetizers are the perfect sponge for mopping up extra sauce and can be made ahead for convenience. Just wrap in foil and reheat in the oven.

—JENNI SHARP MILWAUKEE, WI

PREP: 35 MIN. + STANDING
COOK: 5 MIN./BATCH
MAKES: 8 PANCAKES (¼ CUP SAUCE)

- 3 **cups all-purpose flour**
- 1⅓ **cups boiling water**
- 4 **teaspoons sesame oil**
- 6 **green onions, chopped**
- 1 **teaspoon salt**
- ½ **cup canola oil**

DIPPING SAUCE
- 3 **tablespoons reduced-sodium soy sauce**
- 1 **tablespoon brown sugar**
- 2 **teaspoons minced fresh gingerroot**
- 2 **teaspoons rice vinegar**
- ½ **teaspoon sesame oil**
- ⅛ **teaspoon crushed red pepper flakes**

1. Place flour in a large bowl; stir in boiling water until dough forms a ball. Turn onto a floured surface; knead until smooth and elastic, about 4-6 minutes. Place in a large bowl; cover, let rest for 30 minutes.

2. Divide dough into eight portions; roll each portion into an 8-in. circle. Brush with ½ teaspoon sesame oil; sprinkle with 1 heaping tablespoon of green onion and ⅛ teaspoon salt. Roll up jelly-roll style; holding one end of rope, wrap the dough around, forming a coil, pinching it to seal. Flatten slightly. Roll each coil to ⅛-in. thickness.

3. Using a large skillet, heat 1 tablespoon of the canola oil. Cook the pancakes, one at a time, over medium-high heat for 2-3 minutes on each side or until golden brown.

4. Meanwhile, in a small bowl, combine sauce ingredients. Serve with pancakes.

BARBECUED MEATBALLS

Grape jelly and chili sauce are the secrets that make these meatballs so fantastic. If I am serving them at a party, I make the meatballs and sauce in advance and reheat them right before guests arrive.

—IRMA SCHNUELLE MANITOWOC, WI

PREP: 20 MIN. • **COOK:** 15 MIN.
MAKES: ABOUT 3 DOZEN

- ½ **cup dry bread crumbs**
- ⅓ **cup finely chopped onion**
- ¼ **cup milk**
- 1 **large egg, lightly beaten**
- 1 **tablespoon minced fresh parsley**
- 1 **teaspoon salt**
- 1 **teaspoon Worcestershire sauce**
- ½ **teaspoon pepper**
- 1 **pound lean ground beef (90% lean)**
- ¼ **cup canola oil**
- 1 **bottle (12 ounces) chili sauce**
- 1 **jar (10 ounces) grape jelly**

1. In a large bowl, combine the first eight ingredients. Crumble beef over mixture and mix well. Shape into 1-in. balls. In a large skillet; brown meatballs in oil on all sides.

2. Remove meatballs and drain. In the same skillet, combine chili sauce and jelly; cook and stir over medium heat until jelly has melted. Return meatballs to pan; heat through.

SKILLET NACHOS

My mother gave me a cookbook and the recipe I've used most is for Skillet Nachos. My whole family's on board with this savory snack. For the toppings, think sour cream, tomatoes, jalapeno and red onion.
—**JUDY HUGHES** WAVERLY, KS

START TO FINISH: 30 MIN.
MAKES: 6 SERVINGS

- 1 **pound ground beef**
- 1 **can (14½ ounces) diced tomatoes, undrained**
- 1 **cup fresh or frozen corn, thawed**
- ¾ **cup uncooked instant rice**
- ½ **cup water**
- 1 **envelope taco seasoning**
- ½ **teaspoon salt**
- 1 **cup shredded Colby-Monterey Jack cheese**
- 1 **package (16 ounces) tortilla chips**
   Optional toppings: sour cream, sliced fresh jalapenos, shredded lettuce and lime wedges

1. In a large skillet, cook the beef over medium heat 6-8 minutes or until no longer pink, breaking into crumbles; drain. Stir in tomatoes, corn, rice, water, taco seasoning and salt. Bring to a boil. Reduce the heat; simmer, covered, 8-10 minutes until rice is tender and mixture is slightly thickened.

2. Remove from the heat; sprinkle with cheese. Let stand, covered, 5 minutes or until cheese is melted. Divide tortilla chips among six plates; spoon beef mixture over chips. Serve with toppings as desired.

NOTES

FOCACCIA BARESE

This focaccia has been in our family for several generations, and it has become one of my most requested recipes. Whenever I am invited to a party, I'm not allowed to attend unless I bring it!

—DORA TRAVAGLIO MOUNT PROSPECT, IL

PREP: 30 MIN. + RISING • **BAKE:** 30 MIN.
MAKES: 8 SERVINGS

- 1⅛ teaspoons active dry yeast
- ¾ cup warm water (110° to 115°), divided
- ½ teaspoon sugar
- ⅓ cup mashed potato flakes
- 1½ teaspoons plus 2 tablespoons olive oil, divided
- ¼ teaspoon salt
- 1¾ cups bread flour

TOPPING
- 2 medium tomatoes, thinly sliced
- ¼ cup pitted Greek olives, halved
- 1½ teaspoons minced fresh or dried oregano
- ½ teaspoon coarse salt

1. In a large bowl, dissolve yeast in ½ cup warm water. Add sugar; let stand for 5 minutes. Add the potato flakes, 1½ teaspoons oil, salt, 1 cup flour and remaining water. Beat until smooth. Stir in enough of the remaining flour to form soft dough.

2. Turn onto a floured surface; knead until it is smooth and elastic, about 6-8 minutes. Place in greased bowl, turning once to grease the top. Cover and let rise in a warm place until doubled, about 1 hour. Punch dough down. Cover and let rest for 10 minutes.

3. Place 1 tablespoon olive oil in a 10-in. cast-iron or other ovenproof skillet; tilt pan to evenly coat. Add dough; shape the dough to fit pan. Cover and let rise until doubled, about 30 minutes.

4. With fingertips, make several dimples over top of dough. Brush with remaining tablespoon of oil. Blot the tomato slices with paper towels. Arrange tomato slices and olives over dough; sprinkle with oregano and salt.

5. Bake at 375° for 30-35 minutes or until golden brown.

GENTLEMAN'S WHISKEY BACON JAM

You can slather this smoky jam on pretty much anything. It lasts only a week in the fridge, so I freeze small amounts for quick snacks with crackers.

—COLLEEN DELAWDER HERNDON, VA

PREP: 15 MIN. • **COOK:** 30 MIN. • **MAKES:** 3 CUPS

- 1½ pounds thick-sliced bacon strips, finely chopped
- 8 shallots, finely chopped
- 1 large sweet onion, finely chopped
- 2 garlic cloves, minced
- 1 teaspoon chili powder
- ½ teaspoon paprika
- ¼ teaspoon kosher salt
- ¼ teaspoon pepper
- ½ cup whiskey
- ½ cup maple syrup
- ¼ cup balsamic vinegar
- ½ cup packed brown sugar
  Assorted crackers

1. In a large skillet, cook bacon over medium heat until crisp. Drain on paper towels. Discard all but 2 tablespoons drippings. Add the shallots and onion to the drippings; cook them over medium heat until they are caramelized, stirring occasionally.

2. Stir in garlic; cook 30 seconds. Add the seasonings. Remove from heat; stir in the whiskey and maple syrup. Increase heat to high; bring to a boil, and cook 3 minutes, stirring constantly. Add vinegar and brown sugar; cook another 3 minutes, continuing to stir constantly.

3. Add crumbled bacon; reduce heat to low, and cook 12 minutes, stirring every few minutes. Allow jam to cool slightly. Pulse half of the jam in a food processor until smooth; stir puree into remaining jam. Serve with assorted crackers.

RISE & SHINE

HAWAIIAN HASH

I like the combination of ginger, pineapple and macadamia nuts, plus this dish brings back memories of an island vacation.
—**ROXANNE CHAN** ALBANY, CA

PREP: 20 MIN. • **COOK:** 15 MIN.
MAKES: 6 SERVINGS

- 2 **teaspoons canola oil**
- 1 **teaspoon sesame oil**
- 4 **cups cubed peeled sweet potatoes (about 1 pound)**
- 1 **cup chopped onion**
- ½ **cup chopped sweet red pepper**
- 1 **teaspoon minced fresh gingerroot**
- ¼ **cup water**
- 1 **cup cubed fully cooked ham**
- 1 **cup cubed fresh pineapple or unsweetened pineapple tidbits, drained**
- ¼ **cup salsa verde**
- 1 **teaspoon soy sauce**
- ½ **teaspoon black sesame seeds**
  Chopped fresh cilantro
  Chopped macadamia nuts, optional

1. In a large skillet, heat the oils over medium-high heat. Add sweet potatoes, onion, pepper and gingerroot; cook and stir 5 minutes. Add water. Reduce heat to low; cook, covered, until the potatoes are tender, 8-10 minutes, stirring them occasionally.

2. Stir in next five ingredients; cook and stir over medium-high heat until heated through, about 2 minutes. Top servings with cilantro and, if desired, chopped macadamia nuts.

NOTES

OLD-WORLD PUFF PANCAKE

START TO FINISH: 30 MIN.
MAKES: 4 SERVINGS

- 2 **tablespoons butter**
- 3 **large eggs**
- ¾ **cup whole milk**
- ¾ **cup all-purpose flour**
- 2 **teaspoons sugar**
- 1 **teaspoon ground nutmeg**
  Confectioners' sugar
  Lemon wedges
  Syrup, optional
  Fresh raspberries, optional

1. Place butter in a 10-in. ovenproof skillet; place in a 425° oven for 2-3 minutes or until melted. In a blender, process the eggs, milk, flour, sugar and nutmeg until smooth. Pour into prepared skillet.

2. Bake at 425° for 16-18 minutes or until puffed and browned. Dust with confectioners' sugar. Serve with lemon wedges and, if desired, syrup and raspberries.

My grandmother taught my mom how to make this dish, which was popular during the Depression. At that time, cooks measured ingredients as pinches and dashes, but through the years, accurate amounts were noted. My wife and I continue to enjoy this treat today, particularly for brunch.

—AUTON MILLER PINEY FLATS, TN

MEDITERRANEAN BROCCOLI & CHEESE OMELET

My Italian mother-in-law taught me to make this hearty omelet years ago—she served it for breakfast, lunch and dinner. I often use leftover broccoli from a previous meal.

—MARY LICATA PEMBROKE PINES, FL

START TO FINISH: 30 MIN.
MAKES: 4 SERVINGS

- 2½ cups fresh broccoli florets
- 6 large eggs
- ¼ cup 2% milk
- ½ teaspoon salt
- ¼ teaspoon pepper
- ⅓ cup grated Romano cheese
- ⅓ cup sliced pitted Greek olives
- 1 tablespoon olive oil
  Shaved Romano cheese and minced fresh parsley

1. Preheat broiler. In a large saucepan, place steamer basket over 1 in. of water. Place broccoli in basket. Bring water to a boil. Reduce heat to a simmer; steam, covered, 4-6 minutes or until crisp-tender.

2. In a large bowl, whisk eggs, milk, salt and pepper. Stir in cooked broccoli, grated cheese and olives. Using a 10-in. ovenproof skillet, heat oil over medium heat; pour in egg mixture. Cook, uncovered, 4-6 minutes or until nearly set.

3. Broil 3-4 in. from heat 2-4 minutes or until eggs are completely set. Let stand 5 minutes. Cut into wedges. Sprinkle with shaved cheese and parsley.

GRANDMOTHER'S TOAD IN A HOLE

I have fond memories of my grandmother's Yorkshire pudding wrapped around sausages, a puffy dish that my kids called The Boat. Slather it with some butter and maple syrup.

—SUSAN KIEBOAM STREETSBORO, OH

PREP: 10 MIN. + STANDING • **BAKE:** 25 MIN.
MAKES: 6 SERVINGS

- 3 **large eggs**
- 1 **cup 2% milk**
- ½ **teaspoon salt**
- 1 **cup all-purpose flour**
- 1 **package (12 ounces) uncooked maple breakfast sausage links**
- 3 **tablespoons olive oil**
  Butter and maple syrup, optional

1. Preheat oven to 400°. In a small bowl, whisk eggs, milk and salt. Whisk flour into egg mixture until blended. Let stand 30 minutes. Meanwhile, cook sausage according to package directions; cut each sausage into three pieces.

2. Place oil in a 12-in. nonstick ovenproof skillet. Place in oven 3-4 minutes or until hot. Stir batter and pour into prepared skillet; top with sausage. Bake 20-25 minutes or until golden brown and puffed. Remove from the skillet; cut into wedges. If desired, serve with butter and syrup.

ROASTED VEGETABLE FRITTATA

The great thing about a frittata is that I can make one with whatever I have available in my garden and pantry. The version here uses spring produce to its advantage. I've found that the roasting really intensifies the natural sweetness of the asparagus and onion, and the earthiness of the potatoes.
—**TRISHA KRUSE** EAGLE, ID

PREP: 25 MIN. • **BAKE:** 15 MIN.
MAKES: 6 SERVINGS

- 1 **pound fresh asparagus, trimmed and cut into 2-inch pieces.**
- 2 **small red potatoes, halved and thinly sliced**
- 1½ **cups sliced sweet onion (½ inch thick)**
- 2 **tablespoons olive oil, divided**
- 1 **teaspoon salt, divided**
- ½ **teaspoon pepper, divided**
- 4 **large eggs**
- ½ **cup 2% milk**
- 1 **cup finely chopped, fully cooked ham**
- 3 **garlic cloves, minced**
- ½ **cup shredded part-skim mozzarella cheese**
- ¼ **cup grated Parmesan cheese**
- 2 **tablespoons minced fresh basil**

1. Preheat oven to 450°. In a large bowl, combine asparagus, potatoes and onion. Mix 1 tablespoon oil, ½ teaspoon salt and ¼ teaspoon pepper; drizzle over the vegetables. Toss to coat. Transfer to ungreased baking sheet. Roast 15-20 minutes or until vegetables are golden and tender, stirring halfway.

2. Meanwhile, whisk the eggs, milk and remaining salt and pepper until they are blended.

3. Reduce oven setting to 350°. In a large ovenproof skillet, heat the remaining oil over medium-high heat. Add the ham; cook and stir 2-3 minutes or until lightly browned. Reduce heat to medium. Add the roasted vegetables and garlic; cook 1 minute longer. Pour in egg mixture; sprinkle with cheeses and basil.

4. Bake, uncovered, 15-18 minutes or until eggs are completely set. Let stand 5 minutes. Cut into wedges.

SAUSAGE, EGG & CHEDDAR FARMER'S BREAKFAST

When we're camping, we eat a late breakfast, so this hearty combination of sausage, hash browns and eggs is just right.

—BONNIE ROBERTS NEWAYGO, MI

START TO FINISH: 30 MIN.
MAKES: 4 SERVINGS

- 6 **large eggs**
- ⅓ **cup 2% milk**
- ½ **teaspoon dried parsley flakes**
- ¼ **teaspoon salt**
- 6 **ounces bulk pork sausage**
- 1 **tablespoon butter**
- 1½ **cups frozen cubed hash brown potatoes, thawed**
- ¼ **cup chopped onion**
- 1 **cup shredded cheddar cheese**

1. Whisk eggs, milk, parsley and salt; set aside. In a 9-in. cast-iron or other ovenproof skillet, cook sausage over medium heat until no longer pink; remove and drain. In same skillet, heat butter over medium heat. Add potatoes and onion; cook and stir for 5-7 minutes or until tender. Return sausage to pan.

2. Add the egg mixture; cook and stir until almost set. Sprinkle with cheese. Cover and cook for 1-2 minutes or until cheese is melted.

CAMPFIRE READY

APPLES & CREAM PANCAKE

This recipe is delicious for breakfast or brunch. I usually make a double batch—because everyone wants more! Because we have our own apple orchard, we have plenty of Delicious and Winesap apples on hand for this heartwarming treat.

—RUTH SCHAFER DEFIANCE, OH

START TO FINISH: 25 MIN.
MAKES: 4-6 SERVINGS

- ½ **cup milk**
- 2 **large eggs**
- ½ **cup all-purpose flour**
- ¼ **teaspoon salt**
- 1 **to 2 tablespoons butter**
- ¼ **cup packed brown sugar**
- 3 **ounces cream cheese, softened**
- ½ **cup sour cream**
- ½ **teaspoon vanilla extract**
- 1½ **cups thinly sliced unpeeled apples**
- ¼ **cup chopped walnuts**

1. Preheat oven to 450°. In a small bowl, combine milk, eggs, flour and salt. Beat until smooth. Set a cast-iron or ovenproof skillet in the oven at 450° until hot.
2. Carefully add butter to the skillet; spread over entire bottom. Pour in the batter; bake for 10 minutes or until golden brown.
3. Meanwhile, combine sugar and cream cheese. Blend in sour cream and vanilla. Fill pancake with ¾ cup cream cheese mixture and top with apples. Spread the remaining cream cheese mixture over apples and sprinkle with nuts. Cut into wedges and serve immediately.

PECAN-OATMEAL PANCAKES

When I was a schoolteacher, these hearty pancakes, topped with my favorite syrup and fresh fruit, were the perfect energy booster for hectic days. I still love their nutty flavor.

—FRED SCHWIERSKE MOUNT HOREB, WI

START TO FINISH: 30 MIN.
MAKES: 14-16 PANCAKES

- 1½ **cups quick-cooking oats**
- 1 **cup all-purpose flour**
- 2 **tablespoons brown sugar**
- 2 **teaspoons baking powder**
- ¼ **teaspoon salt**
- 1½ **cups whole milk**
- 2 **large eggs, lightly beaten**
- 2 **tablespoons butter or margarine, melted**
- ½ **cup chopped pecans**

In a bowl, combine the oats, flour, brown sugar, baking powder and salt. Combine milk, eggs and butter; stir into dry ingredients just until blended. Fold in pecans. Pour batter by ¼ cupfuls onto a greased cast-iron skillet or griddle over medium-high heat; turn when bubbles form on top of pancakes. Cook until second side is golden brown.

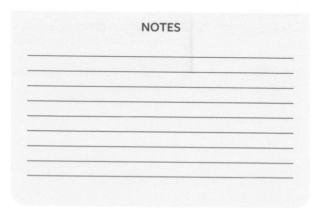

NOTES

CAMPFIRE READY

SIDE-DISH SKILLET

START TO FINISH: 30 MIN.
MAKES: 6 SERVINGS

- 1 **package (12 ounces) pork sausage links**
- 5 **medium apples, (about 1¼ pounds), peeled and quartered**
- 3 **tablespoons brown sugar**
- 1 **tablespoon lemon juice**
- ⅛ **teaspoon salt**

In a heavy 12-in. cast-iron or other ovenproof skillet, cook the sausages over medium-high heat, turning them occasionally, about 10 minutes; drain. Add the apple wedges. Sprinkle them with brown sugar, lemon juice and salt. Cover and cook over medium heat for 10-15 minutes or until apples are tender and sausages are fully cooked.

With its great combination of flavors and ease of preparation, this is one of my go-to dishes to make when we have overnight guests. We like it with scrambled eggs and toast.

—LYNN CRONK INDIANAPOLIS, IN

COUNTRY-STYLE SCRAMBLED EGGS

Here, I added a little color and flavor to ordinary scrambled eggs with some green pepper, onion and red potatoes.

—JOYCE PLATFOOT WAPAKONETA, OH

START TO FINISH: 30 MIN.
MAKES: 4 SERVINGS

- 8 bacon strips, diced
- 2 cups diced red potatoes
- ½ cup chopped onion
- ½ cup chopped green pepper
- 8 large eggs
- ¼ cup milk
- 1 teaspoon salt
- ¼ teaspoon pepper
- 1 cup shredded cheddar cheese

1. In a 9-in. cast-iron or other ovenproof skillet, cook the bacon over medium heat until it is crisp. Using a slotted spoon, remove to paper towels to drain. Cook and stir the potatoes in drippings over medium heat for 12 minutes or until tender. Add the onion and green pepper. Cook and stir for 3-4 minutes or until crisp-tender; drain. Stir in the bacon.

2. In a large bowl, whisk the eggs, milk, salt and pepper; add to skillet. Cook and stir until eggs are completely set. Sprinkle with cheese and stir it in or let stand until melted.

CAMPFIRE READY

CHOCOLATE CHIP DUTCH BABY

I modified a traditional Dutch baby recipe given to me by a friend to come up with this version my family thinks is just terrific. You'll be surprised at how easy it is.

—MARY THOMPSON LACROSSE, WI

START TO FINISH: 30 MIN.
MAKES: 4 SERVINGS

¼ **cup miniature semisweet chocolate chips**
¼ **cup packed brown sugar**

DUTCH BABY

½ **cup all-purpose flour**
2 **large eggs**
½ **cup half-and-half cream**
⅛ **teaspoon ground nutmeg**
  Dash ground cinnamon
3 **tablespoons butter**
  Maple syrup and additional butter, optional

1. Preheat oven to 425°. In a small bowl, combine the chocolate chips and brown sugar; set aside. In another small bowl, beat the flour, eggs, cream, nutmeg and cinnamon until smooth.

2. Place butter in a 9-in. pie plate or an 8-in. cast iron skillet. Heat in oven for 4 minutes or until melted. Pour batter into hot pie plate or skillet. Sprinkle with chocolate chip mixture. Bake for 13-15 minutes or until top edges are golden brown. Serve immediately with syrup and butter if desired.

COUNTRY CORNCAKES

Although we live in a suburban area, we are lucky to have plenty of farms nearby where we purchase fresh homegrown corn. When it's out of season, however, I do substitute canned or frozen corn in this change-of-pace recipe.

—ANNE FREDERICK NEW HARTFORD, NY

PREP: 15 MIN. • **COOK:** 20 MIN.
MAKES: 14 CORNCAKES

- 1½ cups yellow cornmeal
- ¼ cup all-purpose flour
- 1 tablespoon sugar
- 1 teaspoon baking soda
- ½ teaspoon salt
- 1 large egg
- 1½ cups buttermilk
- 2 tablespoons butter, melted
- 1½ cups fresh corn or frozen corn
  Sour cream, optional
- 6 bacon strips, cooked and crumbled, optional
- 2 tablespoons minced chives, optional

1. In a small bowl, combine first five ingredients; make a well in the center. In another bowl, beat the egg, buttermilk and butter; pour into the well and stir just until blended. Gently stir in corn; do not overmix. Cover and let stand for 5 minutes.

2. Pour the batter by ¼ cupfuls onto a greased cast-iron skillet or griddle over medium-high heat. Turn when bubbles form on top, about 2-3 minutes. Cook until second side is golden brown. Top with the sour cream, bacon and chives if desired.

CAMPFIRE
READY

SAUSAGE HASH

PREP: 10 MIN. • **COOK:** 30 MIN.
MAKES: 6 SERVINGS

- 1 **pound bulk pork sausage**
- 1 **medium onion, chopped**
- 2 **medium carrots, grated**
- 1 **medium green pepper, chopped**
- 3 **cups diced cooked potatoes**
- ½ **teaspoon salt**
- ¼ **teaspoon pepper**

In a large skillet, cook the sausage over medium heat until it is no longer pink; drain. Add the onion, carrots and green pepper; cook until tender. Stir in the potatoes, salt and pepper. Reduce heat; cook and stir for 20 minutes or until lightly browned and heated through.

I always keep pork sausage in the freezer, so when I need a quick meal, I turn to this handy recipe. The colorful vegetables give it a perky look to match its flavor.

—VIRGINIA KRITES CRIDERSVILLE, OH

GERMAN APPLE PANCAKE

If you're looking for a pretty dish to make when having brunch guests, consider trying this. Everyone I have served it to has enjoyed it, and it's always been a hit....except one time, that is, when my husband made it following my recipe, which I had written down incorrectly. If you don't leave out the flour like I did, it'll turn out terrific!

—JUDI VAN BEEK LYNDEN, WA

PREP: 15 MIN. • **BAKE:** 20 MIN.
MAKES: 6 SERVINGS

PANCAKE
- 3 **large eggs**
- 1 **cup milk**
- ¾ **cup all-purpose flour**
- ½ **teaspoon salt**
- ⅛ **teaspoon ground nutmeg**
- 3 **tablespoons butter**

TOPPING
- 2 **tart baking apples, peeled and sliced**
- 3 **to 4 tablespoons butter**
- 2 **tablespoons sugar**
  Confectioners' sugar

1. Heat a 10-in. cast-iron skillet in 425° oven. Meanwhile, in a blender, combine eggs, milk, flour, salt and nutmeg; cover and process until smooth.

2. Add butter to hot skillet; return to oven until butter bubbles. Pour batter into skillet. Bake, uncovered, for 20 minutes or until pancake puffs and edges are browned and crisp.

3. For topping, in a skillet, add the apples, butter and sugar; cook and stir over medium heat until apples are tender. Spoon into the baked pancake. Sprinkle with confectioners' sugar. Cut and serve immediately.

LOADED BREAKFAST POTATOES

My children love loaded potatoes in restaurants, so I modified this side dish to make it at home. Using the microwave for the potatoes will save you about 10 minutes. I also cut peeling time by using thin-skinned red potatoes instead of russets.

—TENA KROPP AURORA, IL

START TO FINISH: 30 MIN.
MAKES: 6 SERVINGS

- 1½ **pounds red potatoes, cubed**
- ¼ **pound bacon strips, chopped**
- ¾ **cup cubed fully cooked ham**
- 1 **cup shredded cheddar cheese**
- ½ **teaspoon salt**
- ¼ **teaspoon pepper**
  Sour cream

1. Place the potatoes in a microwave-safe dish and cover with water. Cover and microwave on high for 4-5 minutes or until tender.

2. Meanwhile, in a large skillet, cook bacon over medium heat until crisp. Remove to paper towels with a slotted spoon. Drain potatoes; saute in drippings until lightly browned. Add the ham, cheese, salt, pepper and bacon. Cook and stir over medium heat until cheese is melted. Serve with sour cream.

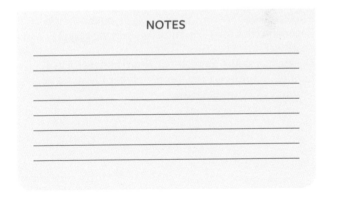

NOTES

CARAMELIZED MUSHROOM & ONION FRITTATA

When I was young, my grandmother used to make buttery sauteed mushrooms for me. Now I enjoy them in a hearty breakfast frittata.

—MELISSA D'ANTONIO POUGHKEEPSIE, NY

PREP: 15 MIN. • **COOK:** 45 MIN.
MAKES: 4 SERVINGS

- 1 **pound sliced fresh mushrooms**
- 1 **medium red onion, chopped**
- 3 **tablespoons butter**
- 3 **tablespoons olive oil**
- 1 **shallot, chopped**
- 1 **garlic clove, minced**
- ½ **cup shredded cheddar cheese**
- ¼ **cup shredded Parmesan cheese**
- 8 **large eggs**
- 3 **tablespoons heavy whipping cream**
- ¼ **teaspoon salt**
- ¼ **teaspoon pepper**

1. In a 10-in. ovenproof skillet, saute mushrooms and onion in butter and oil until softened. Reduce heat to medium-low; cook for 30 minutes or until deep golden brown, stirring occasionally. Add shallot and garlic; cook 1 minute longer.

2. Reduce heat; sprinkle with cheeses. In a large bowl, whisk the eggs, cream, salt and pepper; pour over top. Cover and cook for 4-6 minutes or until the eggs are nearly set.

3. Uncover skillet. Broil 3-4 in. from the heat for 2-3 minutes or until eggs are completely set. Let stand for 5 minutes. Cut into wedges.

HAM & POTATO BREAKFAST

PREP: 10 MIN. • **COOK:** 30 MIN.
MAKES: 6 SERVINGS

- 1 **pound red potatoes, cooked and sliced**
- 3 **tablespoons butter, divided**
- 1½ **cups thinly sliced fresh mushrooms**
- 1 **cup thinly sliced onion**
- 1 **sweet red pepper, cut into thin strips**
- 2 **cups diced fully cooked ham**
- 2 **teaspoons minced fresh garlic**
- ½ **cup minced fresh parsley or basil**
- 1 **tablespoon olive oil**
- 8 **large eggs**
  Salt and pepper to taste
- 1½ **cups shredded cheddar or Swiss cheese**

1. In a 10-in. cast-iron or another ovenproof skillet, brown potatoes in 2 tablespoons butter over medium-high heat; remove and set aside.

2. Using the same skillet, saute the mushrooms, onion, red pepper and ham in the remaining butter until the vegetables are tender. Add the garlic; cook 1 minute longer; drain. Remove and set aside.

3. Using the same skillet, cook the potatoes, ham mixture and parsley in oil over medium-high heat. In a large bowl, beat the eggs, salt and pepper. Pour into skillet; cover and cook for 10-15 minutes or until eggs are nearly set.

4. Broil 5-6 in. from the heat for 2-3 minutes or until eggs are set. Sprinkle with the cheese and broil until melted. Cut into wedges.

Easy and delicious, this dish is appreciated whenever I serve it...breakfast, lunch or dinner. Reheated or cold, the leftovers are always great, too!

—KATIE DREIBELBIS STATE COLLEGE, PA

CAST-IRON PEACH CROSTATA

While the crostata, an open-faced fruit tart, is actually Italian, my own version's peach filling is American all the way.

—LAUREN KNOELKE MILWAUKEE, WI

PREP: 45 MIN. + CHILLING
COOK: 45 MIN.
MAKES: 10 SERVINGS

- 1½ **cups all-purpose flour**
- 2 **tablespoons plus ¾ cup packed brown sugar, divided**
- 1¼ **teaspoons salt, divided**
- ½ **cup cold unsalted butter, cubed**
- 2 **tablespoons shortening**
- 3 **to 5 tablespoons ice water**
- 8 **cups sliced peaches (about 7-8 medium)**
- 1 **tablespoon lemon juice**
- 3 **tablespoons cornstarch**
- ½ **teaspoon ground cinnamon**
- ¼ **teaspoon ground nutmeg**
- 1 **large egg, beaten**
- 2 **tablespoons sliced almonds**
- 1 **tablespoon coarse sugar**
- ⅓ **cup water**
- 1 **cup fresh raspberries, optional**

1. Mix flour, 2 tablespoons brown sugar and 1 teaspoon salt; cut in the butter and shortening until crumbly. Gradually add ice water, tossing with a fork until the dough holds together when pressed. Shape into a disk; wrap in plastic wrap. Refrigerate 1 hour or overnight.

2. Combine peaches and lemon juice. Add remaining brown sugar, cornstarch, spices and remaining salt; toss gently. Let stand about 30 minutes.

3. Preheat the oven to 400°. On a lightly floured surface, roll dough into a 13-in. circle; transfer it to a 10-in. cast-iron skillet, letting the excess hang over the edge. Using a slotted spoon, transfer peaches into pastry, reserving liquid. Fold pastry edge over filling, pleating as you go, leaving center uncovered. Brush the folded pastry with beaten egg; sprinkle with almonds and coarse sugar. Bake until the crust is dark golden and the filling is bubbly, 45-55 minutes.

4. In a small saucepan, combine reserved liquid and water; bring to a boil. Simmer until thickened, 1-2 minutes; serve warm with pie. If desired, top with fresh raspberries.

CAMPER'S BREAKFAST HASH

When we go camping with family and friends, I always prepare this hearty breakfast. And it's a favorite at home, too.

—LINDA KRIVANEK OAK CREEK, WI

START TO FINISH: 25 MIN.
MAKES: 8 SERVINGS

¼ **cup butter, cubed**
2 **packages (20 ounces each) refrigerated shredded hash brown potatoes**
1 **package (7 ounces) frozen fully cooked breakfast sausage links, thawed and cut into ½-inch pieces**
¼ **cup chopped onion**
¼ **cup chopped green pepper**
12 **large eggs, lightly beaten**
 Salt and pepper to taste
1 **cup shredded cheddar cheese**

1. In a deep 12-in. cast-iron or other ovenproof skillet, melt butter. Add the potatoes, sausage, onion and green pepper. Cook, uncovered, over medium heat for 15-20 minutes or until potatoes are lightly browned, turning once.

2. Push potato mixture to the sides of pan. Pour eggs into the center of the pan. Cook and stir over medium heat until the eggs are completely set. Season with salt and pepper. Reduce the heat; stir eggs into potato mixture. Top with cheese; cover and cook for 1-2 minutes or until cheese is melted.

BLACK BEAN &
WHITE CHEDDAR FRITTATA

This is one of my favorite comfort foods for breakfast or even a quick dinner. I like to make it with mild lime salsa, but if you're looking for something with a bit more kick, use hot salsa or add some chipotle pepper.

—AYSHA SCHURMAN AMMON, ID

PREP: 20 MIN. • **COOK:** 15 MIN.
MAKES: 6 SERVINGS

- 6 large eggs
- 3 large egg whites
- ¼ cup salsa
- 1 tablespoon minced fresh parsley
- ¼ teaspoon salt
- ¼ teaspoon pepper
- 1 tablespoon olive oil
- ⅓ cup finely chopped green pepper
- ⅓ cup finely chopped sweet red pepper
- 3 green onions, finely chopped
- 2 garlic cloves, minced
- 1 cup canned black beans, rinsed and drained
- ½ cup shredded white cheddar cheese
  Optional toppings: minced fresh cilantro, sliced ripe olives and additional salsa

1. Preheat broiler. In a large bowl, whisk the first six ingredients until blended.
2. In a 10-in. ovenproof skillet, heat oil over medium-high heat. Add peppers and green onions; cook and stir 3-4 minutes or until peppers are tender. Add garlic; cook 1 minute longer. Stir in beans. Reduce heat to medium; stir in egg mixture. Cook, uncovered, 4-6 minutes or until nearly set. Sprinkle with cheese.
3. Broil 3-4 in. from heat 3-4 minutes or until light golden brown and eggs are completely set. Let stand 5 minutes. Cut into wedges. If desired, serve with toppings.

HELPFUL HINT

Cooking for someone with diabetes? This dish is a smart choice. The diabetic exchanges are equal to 2 medium-fat meat, ½ starch and ½ fat.

SHAKSHUKA

Shakshuka is a dish made of poached eggs, tomatoes, peppers and cumin. I learned it while traveling, and its been my favorite way to eat eggs since.
—**EZRA WEEKS** CALGARY, AB

START TO FINISH: 30 MIN.
MAKES: 4 SERVINGS

- 2 **tablespoons olive oil**
- 1 **medium onion, chopped**
- 1 **garlic clove, minced**
- 1 **teaspoon ground cumin**
- 1 **teaspoon pepper**
- ½ **to 1 teaspoon chili powder**
- ½ **teaspoon salt**
- 1 **teaspoon Sriracha Asian hot chili sauce or hot pepper sauce, optional**
- 2 **medium tomatoes, chopped**
- 4 **large eggs**
  Chopped fresh cilantro
  Whole pita breads, toasted

1. In a large skillet, heat the oil over medium heat. Add onion; cook and stir 4-6 minutes or until tender. Add garlic, seasonings and, if desired, hot chili sauce; cook 30 seconds longer. Add tomatoes; cook 3-5 minutes or until the mixture is thickened, stirring it occasionally.

2. With back of spoon, make four wells in vegetable mixture; break an egg into each well. Cook, covered, 4-6 minutes or until egg whites are completely set and yolks begin to thicken but are not hard. Sprinkle with cilantro; serve with pita bread.

NOTES

SAUSAGE JOHNNYCAKE

Here is a nice, hearty breakfast with plenty of old-fashioned flair. I serve it to my bed-and-breakfast customers who love the cake's savory surprise in the middle and the syrup topping. It's a great way to start the day!

—**LORRAINE GUYN** CALGARY, AB

PREP: 20 MIN. • **BAKE:** 30 MIN.
MAKES: 6 SERVINGS

- 1 **cup cornmeal**
- 2 **cups buttermilk**
- 12 **uncooked breakfast sausage links**
- 1⅓ **cups all-purpose flour**
- ¼ **cup sugar**
- 1½ **teaspoons baking powder**
- ½ **teaspoon baking soda**
- ½ **teaspoon salt**
- ⅓ **cup shortening**
- 1 **large egg, lightly beaten**
- ½ **teaspoon vanilla extract**
  Maple syrup

1. In a small bowl, combine the cornmeal and buttermilk; let stand for 10 minutes.

2. Meanwhile, in a 9-in. cast-iron skillet over medium heat, cook the sausage until no longer pink; drain on paper towels. Arrange eight links in a spoke-like pattern in the same skillet or a greased 9-in. deep-dish pie plate. Cut the remaining links in half; place them between the whole sausages.

3. In a large bowl, combine flour, sugar, baking powder, baking soda and salt. Cut in shortening until mixture resembles coarse crumbs.

4. Stir the egg and vanilla into the cornmeal mixture; add to the dry ingredients; stir just until blended. Pour batter over the sausages.

5. Bake at 400° for 30-35 minutes or until a toothpick inserted in the center comes out clean. Serve warm with syrup.

FREEZE OPTION *Wrap the Johnnycakes in foil; transfer to a resealable plastic freezer bag. May be frozen for up to 3 months. To use, remove the foil and thaw at room temperature. Serve Johnnycakes warm with syrup.*

RING THE
DINNER BELL

SKILLET-ROASTED LEMON CHICKEN WITH POTATOES

This is a meal I have my students make in our nutrition unit. It offers a delicious lemon-herb flavor and is simple to make.
—MINDY ROTTMUND LANCASTER, PA

PREP: 20 MIN. • **BAKE:** 25 MIN.
MAKES: 4 SERVINGS

- 1 **tablespoon olive oil, divided**
- 1 **medium lemon, thinly sliced**
- 4 **garlic cloves, minced and divided**
- ¼ **teaspoon grated lemon peel**
- ½ **teaspoon salt, divided**
- ¼ **teaspoon pepper, divided**
- 8 **boneless skinless chicken thighs (4 ounces each)**
- ¼ **teaspoon dried rosemary, crushed**
- 1 **pound fingerling potatoes, halved lengthwise**
- 8 **cherry tomatoes**
  Fresh parsley, minced

1. Preheat oven to 450°. Grease a 10-in. cast iron or other ovenproof skillet with 1 teaspoon oil. Arrange the lemon slices in a single layer in the skillet.

2. Combine 1 teaspoon oil, half of the garlic, the lemon peel, ¼ teaspoon salt and ⅛ teaspoon pepper; rub over the chicken. Place the chicken over the lemon slices.

3. Combine rosemary and remaining oil, garlic, salt and pepper. Add potatoes and tomatoes; toss to coat. Arrange over chicken. Bake, uncovered, 25-30 minutes or until chicken is no longer pink and potatoes are tender. Sprinkle with parsley before serving.

BEEF TACO SKILLET

Busy day? Save time and money with a stovetop supper the whole family will love. It calls for handy convenience products, so it can be on the table in minutes.

—KELLY RODER FAIRFAX, VA

START TO FINISH: 20 MIN.
MAKES: 6 SERVINGS

- 1 **pound ground beef**
- 1 **small red onion, chopped**
- 1 **can (15¼ ounces) whole kernel corn, drained**
- 10 **corn tortillas (6 inches), cut into 1-inch pieces**
- 1 **bottle (8 ounces) taco sauce**
- 1¼ **cups shredded cheddar cheese, divided**
   Hot pepper sauce, optional

In a large skillet, cook beef and onion over medium heat until meat is no longer pink; drain. Add the corn, tortillas, taco sauce and 1 cup cheese; heat through. Sprinkle with remaining cheese. Serve with pepper sauce if desired.

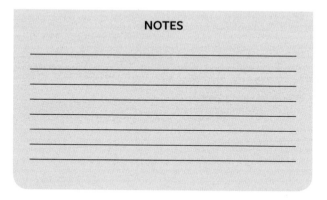

NOTES

DEEP-DISH SAUSAGE PIZZA

My grandma made the tastiest snacks for us whenever we stayed over at her farm. Her pizza, hot from the oven, was covered with cheese and had fragrant herbs in the crust. Now this pizza is frequently a meal for my husband and me and our two young daughters.

—MICHELE MADDEN
WASHINGTON COURT HOUSE, OH

PREP: 30 MIN. + RISING
BAKE: 30 MIN. + STANDING
MAKES: 8 SLICES

- 1 package (¼ ounce) active dry yeast
- ⅔ cup warm water (110° to 115°)
- 1¾ to 2 cups all-purpose flour
- ¼ cup vegetable oil
- 1 teaspoon each dried oregano, basil and marjoram
- ½ teaspoon garlic salt
- ½ teaspoon onion salt

TOPPINGS
- 4 cups shredded part-skim mozzarella cheese, divided
- 2 medium green peppers, chopped
- 1 large onion, chopped
- ½ teaspoon each dried oregano, basil and marjoram
- 1 tablespoon olive oil
- 1 cup grated Parmesan cheese
- 1 pound bulk pork sausage, cooked and drained
- 1 can (28 ounces) diced tomatoes, well drained
- 2 ounces sliced pepperoni

1. In a large bowl, dissolve yeast in warm water. Add 1 cup flour, oil and seasonings; beat until smooth. Add enough remaining flour to form a soft dough.

2. Turn dough onto a floured surface; knead until smooth and elastic, about 6-8 minutes. Place in a greased bowl; turn once to grease the top. Cover and let rise in a warm place until doubled, about 1 hour.

3. Punch dough down; roll out into a 15-in. circle. Transfer to a well-greased 12-in. heavy ovenproof skillet or round baking pan, letting the dough drape over the edges. Sprinkle with 1 cup of mozzarella.

4. In another skillet, saute green peppers, onion and seasonings in oil until tender; drain. Layer half of the vegetable mixture over the crust. Layer with half of the Parmesan, sausage and tomatoes. Sprinkle with 2 cups mozzarella. Repeat layers. Fold the crust over to form an edge.

5. Bake at 400° for 20 minutes. Sprinkle with the pepperoni and the remaining mozzarella. Bake for 10-15 minutes longer or until the crust is browned. Let stand for 10 minutes before slicing.

SEASONED CRAB CAKES

These scrumptious crab cakes won first place at the National Hard Crab Derby. I entered them on a whim after trying many crab cake recipes for my family.

—BETSY HEDEMAN TIMONIUM, MD

PREP: 20 MIN. + CHILLING • **COOK:** 10 MIN.
MAKES: 8 CRAB CAKES

- 3 **cans (6 ounces each) crabmeat, drained, flaked and cartilage removed**
- 1 **cup cubed bread**
- 2 **large eggs**
- 3 **tablespoons mayonnaise**
- 3 **tablespoons half-and-half cream**
- 1 **tablespoon lemon juice**
- 1 **tablespoon butter, melted**
- 1½ **teaspoons seafood seasoning**
- 1 **teaspoon Worcestershire sauce**
- 1 **teaspoon salt**
- ½ **cup dry bread crumbs**
- ½ **cup canola oil**

1. In a large bowl, combine the crab and bread cubes. In another bowl, whisk eggs, mayonnaise, cream, lemon juice, butter, seafood seasoning, Worcestershire sauce and salt. Add to the crab mixture and mix gently (mixture will be moist).

2. Place bread crumbs in a shallow dish. Drop crab mixture by ⅓ cupfuls into crumbs; shape each into a ¾-in.-thick patty. Carefully turn to coat. Cover and refrigerate for at least 2 hours.

3. Heat oil in a large skillet; cook crab cakes for 4-5 minutes on each side or until golden brown and crispy.

TURKEY A LA KING

This is a great way to use up leftover turkey. You might want to make extra turkey just to make sure you have leftovers!

—MARY GAYLORD BALSAM LAKE, WI

START TO FINISH: 25 MIN.
MAKES: 6 SERVINGS

- 1 medium onion, chopped
- ¾ cup sliced celery
- ¼ cup diced green pepper
- ¼ cup butter, cubed
- ¼ cup all-purpose flour
- 1 teaspoon sugar
- 1½ cups chicken broth
- ¼ cup half-and-half cream
- 3 cups cubed cooked turkey or chicken
- 1 can (4 ounces) sliced mushrooms, drained
- 6 pastry shells or pieces of toast

In a large skillet, saute the onion, celery and green pepper in butter until tender. Stir in the flour and sugar until a paste forms. Gradually stir in broth. Bring to a boil; boil 1 minute or until thickened. Reduce heat. Add the cream, turkey and mushrooms; heat through. Serve in pastry shells or over toast.

NOTES

SKILLET CHICKEN CORDON BLEU

A dear friend from my high school days shared this recipe with me. You might think something that looks this fancy must be complicated to make, but it's really quite easy!

—**NANCY ZIMMERER** MEDINA, OH

PREP: 10 MIN. • **COOK:** 35 MIN.
MAKES: 4 SERVINGS

- 4 **boneless skinless chicken breast halves (4 ounces each)**
- 4 **thin slices fully cooked ham**
- 4 **thin slices Swiss cheese**
- 3 **tablespoons all-purpose flour**
- 1 **teaspoon paprika**
- ⅓ **cup butter**
- ½ **cup white grape juice**
- 1 **chicken bouillon cube**
- 1 **cup heavy whipping cream**
- 1 **tablespoon cornstarch**

1. Flatten chicken to ¼-in. thickness. Top each with a slice of ham and cheese, folding the ham and cheese as needed to fit. Roll up tightly and secure with toothpicks. In a shallow bowl, combine the flour and paprika. Coat chicken with flour mixture.

2. In a large skillet over medium heat, melt butter. Cook chicken for 5 minutes on each side or no longer pink. Add grape juice and bouillon. Reduce heat; cover and simmer for 30 minutes or until chicken is tender.

3. Remove the chicken and keep warm. In a small bowl, combine cream and cornstarch until smooth. Gradually stir into the pan juices. Bring to a boil; cook and stir for 2 minutes or until thickened. Serve with chicken.

KIELBASA CABBAGE SKILLET

Spicy kielbasa sausage and plentiful cabbage and potatoes give this dish a pleasing, Old World flavor. My husband never liked cabbage before I made this, but now he does!

—ROMAINE WETZEL RONKS, PA

PREP: 10 MIN. • **COOK:** 1¼ HOURS
MAKES: 4 SERVINGS

- ½ **pound smoked kielbasa or smoked Polish sausage, cut into ½-inch slices**
- 2 **tablespoons butter, divided**
- ½ **large head cabbage (2 pounds), coarsely chopped**
- 1 **medium onion, chopped**
- 2 **cans (8 ounces each) tomato sauce**
- ¼ **cup sugar**
- 1 **tablespoon paprika**
- 2 **large potatoes, peeled and cubed**

1. In a large enameled cast-iron or other ovenproof skillet, brown the sausage in 1 tablespoon butter; remove and set aside. In the same pan, saute cabbage and onions in the remaining butter until the onions are tender.

2. In a small bowl, combine the tomato sauce, sugar and paprika; pour over the cabbage mixture. Bring to a boil. Reduce heat; cover and simmer for 20 minutes. Add the potatoes and reserved sausage. Cover and simmer for 30 minutes or until the potatoes are tender.

BLACKENED HALIBUT

START TO FINISH: 25 MIN.
MAKES: 4 SERVINGS

- 2 **tablespoons garlic powder**
- 1 **tablespoon salt**
- 1 **tablespoon onion powder**
- 1 **tablespoon dried oregano**
- 1 **tablespoon dried thyme**
- 1 **tablespoon cayenne pepper**
- 1 **tablespoon pepper**
- 2½ **teaspoons paprika**
- 4 **halibut fillets (4 ounces each)**
- 2 **tablespoons butter**

1. In a large resealable plastic bag, combine the first eight ingredients. Add fillets, two at a time, and shake to coat.

2. In a large cast-iron skillet, cook fillets in butter over medium heat for 3-4 minutes on each side or until fish flakes easily with a fork.

Serve these spicy fillets with garlic mashed potatoes, hot, crusty bread and a crisp salad to lure in your crew. This is what my family eats when we want to celebrate.

—BRENDA WILLIAMS SANTA MARIA, CA

CAMPFIRE READY

SKILLET CHICKEN FAJITAS

Fresh flavor with a flair describes this quick and easy recipe. Fajitas are great for hot summer evenings when you want to serve something fun and tasty, yet keep cooking to a minimum. Try topping them with sour cream, guacamole or both. My family loves them!

—LINDSAY ST. JOHN PLAINFIELD, IN

START TO FINISH: 30 MIN.
MAKES: 6 SERVINGS

- ¼ cup lime juice
- 1 garlic clove, minced
- 1 teaspoon chili powder
- ½ teaspoon salt
- ½ teaspoon ground cumin
- 2 tablespoons olive oil, divided
- 1½ pounds boneless skinless chicken breasts, cut into strips
- 1 medium onion, cut into thin wedges
- ½ medium sweet red pepper, cut into strips
- ½ medium yellow pepper, cut into strips
- ½ medium green pepper, cut into strips
- ½ cup salsa
- 12 flour tortillas (8 inches), warmed
- 1½ cups shredded cheddar cheese or Monterey Jack cheese

1. Mix the first five ingredients and 1 tablespoon of the oil. Add the chicken; toss to coat. Let stand 15 minutes.

2. In a large skillet, heat the remaining oil over medium-high heat; saute onion and peppers until crisp-tender, 3-4 minutes. Remove from pan.

3. In same skillet, saute chicken mixture until no longer pink, 3-4 minutes. Stir in salsa and pepper mixture; heat through. Serve in tortillas. Sprinkle with cheese.

CHEESY PIZZA ROLLS

The cast-iron skillet browns these delicious rolls to perfection. My family can't get enough. Use whatever pizza toppings your family likes best.

—**DOROTHY SMITH** EL DORADO, AR

PREP: 15 MIN. • **BAKE:** 25 MIN.
MAKES: 8 APPETIZERS

- 1 **loaf (1 pound) frozen pizza dough, thawed**
- ½ **cup pasta sauce**
- 1 **cup shredded part-skim mozzarella cheese, divided**
- 1 **cup coarsely chopped pepperoni (about 64 slices)**
- ½ **pound bulk Italian sausage, cooked and crumbled**
- ¼ **cup grated Parmesan cheese**
  Minced fresh basil, optional
  Crushed red pepper flakes, optional

1. Preheat oven to 400°. On a lightly floured surface, roll dough into a 16x10-in. rectangle. Brush with pasta sauce to within ½ in. of edges.

2. Sprinkle with ½ cup mozzarella cheese, pepperoni, sausage and parmesan. Roll up jelly-roll style, starting with a long side; pinch seam to seal. Cut into eight slices. Place in a greased 9-in. cast-iron skillet or greased 9-in. round baking pan, cut side down.

3. Bake 20 minutes; sprinkle with remaining mozzarella cheese. Bake until golden brown, 5-10 more minutes. If desired, serve with minced fresh basil and crushed red pepper flakes.

SPANISH RICE WITH GROUND BEEF

I don't know the origin of this recipe, but it's been in my family for a long time. I can remember eating it often as a little girl.

—**BEVERLY AUSTIN** FULTON, MO

PREP: 5 MIN. • **COOK:** 30 MIN.
MAKES: 6-8 SERVINGS

- 1 **pound ground beef**
- 1 **cup chopped onion**
- ½ **cup chopped green pepper**
- 1 **garlic clove, minced**
- 1 **tablespoon chili powder**
- 1 **bottle (32 ounces) tomato or vegetable juice**
- 1 **cup uncooked long grain rice**
- ½ **teaspoon salt**

In a skillet, brown ground beef; drain. Stir in the onion, green pepper, garlic and chili powder. Cook and stir until the vegetables are tender. Stir in the remaining ingredients; bring to a boil. Reduce the heat; cover and simmer for 20-30 minutes or until the rice is tender and most of the liquid is absorbed.

NOTES

SKILLET CHICKEN STEW

It's been 20 years since I adapted this from a recipe for beef stew. We like it so much that, in all that time, I have never changed any ingredients or amounts—unless it was to double them!

—VALERIE JORDAN KINGMONT, WV

PREP: 15 MIN. • **COOK:** 25 MIN.
MAKES: 4-6 SERVINGS

- ⅓ **cup all-purpose flour**
- ½ **teaspoon salt**
  Dash pepper
- 1½ **pounds boneless skinless chicken breasts, cut into 1-inch pieces**
- 3 **tablespoons butter**
- 1 **medium onion, sliced**
- 3 **celery ribs, sliced**
- 2 **medium potaotes, peeled and cut into ¾-inch cubes**
- 3 **medium carrots, cut into ¼-inch slices**
- 1 **cup chicken broth**
- ½ **teaspoon dried thyme**
- 1 **tablespoon ketchup**
- 1 **tablespoon cornstarch**

1. In a large resealable plastic bag, combine flour, salt and pepper. Add the chicken, a few pieces at a time, and shake to coat.

2. In a large skillet, melt butter; cook the chicken until chicken juices run clear. Add onion and celery; cook for 3 minutes. Stir in potatoes and carrots.

3. In a small bowl, combine the broth, thyme, ketchup and cornstarch; stir into skillet. Bring to a boil. Reduce heat; cover and simmer for 15-20 minutes or until the vegetables are tender.

HELPFUL HINT

A "dash" is a small amount of seasoning added with a quick downward stroke of the hand—somewhere between $\frac{1}{16}$ and a scant $\frac{1}{8}$ teaspoon.

BLACKENED CATFISH WITH MANGO AVOCADO SALSA

A delightful and tasty rub makes this quick recipe fantastic. While the fish is sitting to allow the flavors to blend, you can assemble the salsa. My family thinks this is marvelous.

—LAURA FISHER WESTFIELD, MA

PREP: 20 MIN. + CHILLING • **COOK:** 10 MIN.
MAKES: 4 SERVINGS (2 CUPS SALSA)

- 2 teaspoons dried oregano
- 2 teaspoons ground cumin
- 2 teaspoons paprika
- 2¼ teaspoons pepper, divided
- ¾ teaspoon salt, divided
- 4 catfish fillets (6 ounces each)
- 1 medium mango, peeled and cubed
- 1 medium ripe avocado, peeled and cubed
- ⅓ cup finely chopped red onion
- 2 tablespoons minced fresh cilantro
- 2 tablespoons lime juice
- 2 teaspoons olive oil

1. Combine the oregano, cumin, paprika, 2 teaspoons pepper and ½ teaspoon salt; rub over fillets. Refrigerate for at least 30 minutes.

2. Meanwhile, in a small bowl, combine the mango, avocado, red onion, cilantro, lime juice and the remaining salt and pepper. Chill until serving.

3. In a large cast-iron skillet, cook the fillets in oil over medium heat for 5-7 minutes on each side or until fish flakes easily with a fork. Serve with salsa.

SAUSAGE & VEGETABLE SKILLET

START TO FINISH: 20 MIN.
MAKES: 4 SERVINGS

- 1 **pound fresh Italian sausage links**
- 2 **tablespoons canola oil**
- 2 **cups cubed yellow summer squash**
- 1 **cup chopped green onions**
- 3 **to 4 garlic cloves, minced**
- 3 **cups chopped tomatoes**
- 4 **teaspoons Worcestershire sauce**
- ⅛ **teaspoon cayenne pepper**

In a large skillet over medium heat, cook the sausage in oil until a thermometer reads 160°; drain. When cool enough to handle, cut into ½-inch pieces. Return to the pan. Add squash and onions; cook for 3 minutes. Add garlic; cook 1 minute longer. Stir in the tomatoes, Worcestershire sauce and cayenne pepper; heat through.

This hearty stovetop entree has been a family favorite for years. The variety of vegetables makes this dish colorful and attractive— and the cooking time can't be beat!

—RUBY WILLIAMS BOGALUSA, LA

CHILI SKILLET

Like most farmers, my husband loves chili. And with all of the vegetables, cheese and meat in it, this quick dish makes a real meal-in-one. I serve it frequently in fall and winter. Our two small boys don't care for the olives in this recipe—but the rest they eat right up!

—**KATHERINE BROWN** FREDERICKTOWN, OH

PREP: 10 MIN. • **COOK:** 35 MIN.
MAKES: 4 SERVINGS

- 1 **pound ground beef**
- 1 **cup chopped onion**
- ½ **cup chopped green pepper**
- 1 **garlic clove, minced**
- 1 **can (16 ounces) kidney beans, rinsed and drained**
- 1 **cup tomato juice**
- ½ **cup water**
- 4 **teaspoons chili powder**
- 1 **teaspoon dried oregano**
- 1 **teaspoon salt**
- ½ **cup uncooked long grain rice**
- 1 **cup canned or frozen corn**
- ½ **cup sliced ripe olives**
- 1 **cup shredded cheddar or Monterey Jack cheese**
  Thinly sliced green onions, optional

1. In a large skillet over medium heat, cook beef, onion, pepper and garlic until the meat is no longer pink; drain. Add the next seven ingredients; simmer, covered, until rice is tender, about 25 minutes.

2. Stir in corn and olives; cover and cook 5 minutes more. Sprinkle with cheese; cook, covered, until the cheese is melted, about 5 minutes. If desired, top with green onions.

DINER CORNED BEEF HASH

I created my hash to taste like a dish from a Northern Arizona restaurant we always loved. We round it out with eggs and toast made from homemade bread.

—DENISE CHELPKA PHOENIX, AZ

PREP: 10 MIN. • **COOK:** 25 MIN.
MAKES: 4 SERVINGS

1¼ pounds potatoes (about 3 medium),
   cut into ½-inch cubes
3 tablespoons butter
¾ cup finely chopped celery
¾ pound cooked corned beef,
   cut into ½-inch cubes (about 2½ cups)
4 green onions, chopped
¼ teaspoon pepper
   Dash ground cloves
2 tablespoons minced fresh cilantro

1. Place the potatoes in a saucepan; add the water to cover. Bring to a boil. Reduce heat; cook, uncovered, 6-8 minutes or just until tender. Drain.

2. In a large skillet, heat butter over medium-high heat. Add celery; cook and stir 4-6 minutes or until crisp-tender. Add the potatoes; cook for 6-8 minutes or until lightly browned, turning occasionally. Stir in the corned beef; cook for 1-2 minutes or until heated through. Sprinkle with green onions, pepper and cloves; cook 1-2 minutes longer. Stir in cilantro.

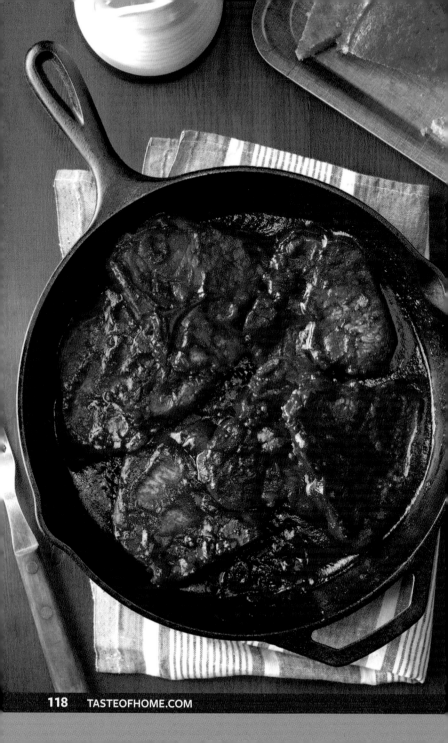

OVEN-BARBECUED PORK CHOPS

My mother has fixed this recipe for years and now I prepare it for my family. The chops are delicious; served with scalloped potatoes and home-baked bread, they're even better!

—TERESA KING WHITTIER, CA

PREP: 10 MIN. • **BAKE:** 40 MIN.
MAKES: 6-8 SERVINGS

- 6 to 8 loin or rib pork chops (¾ inch thick)
- 1 tablespoon Worcestershire sauce
- 2 tablespoons vinegar
- 2 teaspoons brown sugar
- ½ teaspoon pepper
- ½ teaspoon chili powder
- ½ teaspoon paprika
- ¾ cup ketchup
- ⅓ cup hot water

Preheat oven to 375°. Place chops, overlapping slightly if necessary, in a large cast-iron or other ovenproof skillet. Combine remaining ingredients; pour over meat. Bake, uncovered, 40 minutes, turning chops halfway through. through.

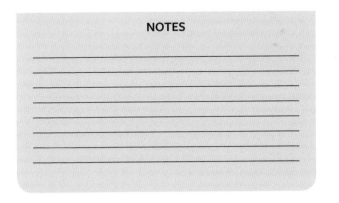

NOTES

GRAM'S FRIED CHICKEN

As a boy, I wolfed down my grandmother's fried chicken. I never knew how she made it, but my recipe using crispy potato flakes comes pretty close.

—DAVID NELSON LINCOLNTON, NC

PREP: 20 MIN. + CHILLING • **COOK:** 10 MIN.
MAKES: 4 SERVINGS

- 1 **large egg**
- 1 **cup 2% milk**
- 2 **cups mashed potato flakes**
- 1 **tablespoon garlic powder**
- 1 **tablespoon each dried oregano, parsley flakes and minced onion**
- ½ **teaspoon salt**
- ¼ **teaspoon coarsely ground pepper**
- 4 **boneless skinless chicken breast halves (6 ounces each)**
  Oil for frying

1. In a shallow bowl, whisk egg and milk. In another shallow bowl, toss the potato flakes with seasonings. Remove half of the mixture and reserve (for a second coat of breading).

2. Pound chicken with a meat mallet to ½-in. thickness. Dip chicken in the egg mixture, then in potato mixture, patting to help the coating adhere. Arrange the chicken in an even layer on a large plate. Cover chicken and the remaining egg mixture; refrigerate for 1 hour. Discard remaining used potato mixture.

3. In a deep 12-in. skillet, heat ½ in. of oil over medium heat to 350°. For the second coat of breading, dip chicken in the remaining egg mixture, then in the unused potato mixture; pat to coat. Fry chicken 4-5 minutes on each side or until golden brown and the chicken is no longer pink. Drain on paper towels.

MAPLE-GLAZED PORK CHOPS

Everyone cleaned their plates when my mother made these succulent, tangy sweet pork chops when I was growing up. Now, I get the same results when I serve them to my family. I like to pair them with applesauce and au gratin potatoes.

—CHERYL MILLER FORT COLLINS, CO

START TO FINISH: 25 MIN.
MAKES: 4 SERVINGS

- ½ cup all-purpose flour
  Salt and pepper to taste
- 4 bone-in pork loin chops (7 ounces each)
- 2 tablespoons butter
- ¼ cup cider vinegar
- ⅓ cup maple syrup
- 1 tablespoon cornstarch
- 3 tablespoons water
- ⅔ cup packed brown sugar

1. In a large resealable plastic bag, combine flour, salt and pepper. Add the pork chops and shake to coat. In a large skillet, cook chops in butter over medium heat for 4-5 minutes on each side or until a thermometer reads 145°. Remove and keep warm.

2. In the same skillet, bring the vinegar to a boil. Reduce heat; add maple syrup. Cover and cook for 10 minutes. Combine cornstarch and water until smooth; gradually add to maple mixture. Bring to a boil; cook and stir for 2 minutes or until thickened.

3. Place chops on a broiler pan; sprinkle with brown sugar. Broil 4 in. from the heat for 1-2 minutes or until sugar is melted. Drizzle with maple glaze.

OVEN SWISS STEAK

This recipe is a great way to use round steak and it picks up fabulous flavor from one of my favorite herbs—tarragon.
—**LORNA DICKAU** VANDERHOOF, BC

PREP: 30 MIN. • **BAKE:** 1¼ HOURS
MAKES: 6 SERVINGS

- 8 **bacon strips**
- 2 **pounds beef top round steak (¾ inch thick)**
- 2 **cups sliced fresh mushrooms**
- 1 **can (14½ ounces) diced tomatoes, undrained**
- ½ **cup chopped onion**
- 1 **to 2 teaspoons dried tarragon**
- 2 **tablespoons cornstarch**
- 2 **tablespoons water**
- 1 **cup heavy whipping cream**
  Minced fresh parsley, optional

1. Preheat the oven to 325°. In a large ovenproof skillet, cook the bacon over medium heat until crisp. Remove to paper towels to drain, reserving ¼ cup of drippings. Crumble bacon and set aside.

2. Trim beef; cut into serving-size pieces. Brown on both sides in drippings. Top meat with mushrooms, tomatoes and onion. Sprinkle with the tarragon and bacon. Cover and bake for 1¼ to 1¾ hours or until the meat is tender, basting twice.

3. Remove the meat to a serving platter; keep warm. Combine cornstarch and water until smooth; add to skillet. Bring to a boil; cook and stir for 2 minutes or until thickened. Reduce heat; stir in cream. Simmer, uncovered, for 3-4 minutes or until heated through. Return meat to skillet and turn to coat with sauce. If desired, sprinkle with parsley.

MEXICAN TURKEY SKILLET

This family-friendly main dish with turkey, black beans and vegetables has a rich Mexican flavor that may seem indulgent, but it's delightfully light. It cooks in one skillet, so it's a snap to clean up for a weeknight supper.

—*TASTE OF HOME* **TEST KITCHEN**

PREP: 20 MIN. • **BAKE:** 30 MIN.
MAKES: 8 SERVINGS

- **1 pound lean ground turkey**
- **1 cup chopped zucchini**
- **½ cup chopped sweet red pepper**
- **2 teaspoons canola oil**
- **2 cups cooked rice**
- **1 can (15 ounces) black beans, rinsed and drained**
- **1 can (14½ ounces) Mexican stewed tomatoes**
- **1 can (8 ounces) tomato sauce**
- **½ teaspoon ground cumin**
- **¼ teaspoon salt**
- **¼ teaspoon pepper**
- **1 cup shredded reduced-fat Mexican cheese blend**
  Chopped avocado, optional

1. Preheat oven to 350°. In a large nonstick ovenproof skillet, cook turkey over medium heat until no longer pink; drain. Set turkey aside. In the same skillet, saute the zucchini and red pepper in oil for 2 minutes or until crisp-tender.

2. Stir in the turkey, rice, beans, tomatoes, tomato sauce, cumin, salt and pepper. Cover and bake for 30 minutes. Sprinkle with cheese. Let stand for 5 minutes before serving. Garnish with avocado if desired.

SPINACH SKILLET BAKE

Over the years, I have tried to instill a love of cooking in our seven children. And along the way we've enjoyed a variety of delicious recipes, including this one.
—**NANCY ROBAIDEK** KRAKOW, WI

PREP: 30 MIN. • **BAKE:** 20 MIN.
MAKES: 4-6 SERVINGS

- 1 **pound ground beef**
- 1 **medium onion, chopped**
- 1 **package (10 ounces) frozen chopped spinach, thawed and squeezed dry**
- 1 **can (4 ounces) mushroom stems and pieces, drained**
- 1 **teaspoon garlic salt**
- 1 **teaspoon dried basil**
- ¼ **cup butter**
- ¼ **cup all-purpose flour**
- ½ **teaspoon salt**
- 2 **cups milk**
- 1 **cup shredded Monterey Jack cheese or part-skim mozzarella cheese**
  Biscuits, optional

1. In a 10-in. cast-iron or other ovenproof skillet, cook beef and onion over medium heat until no longer pink; drain. Add the spinach, mushrooms, garlic salt and basil. Cover and cook for 5 minutes.

2. In a saucepan, melt butter over medium heat. Stir in the flour and salt until smooth. Gradually add milk. bring to a boil; cook and stir for 2 minutes or until thickened. Stir in cheese. Pour over meat mixture; mix well. Reduce heat; cook, covered, until heated through. If desired, serve with biscuits.

TEST KITCHEN TIP *To avoid ending up with lumps in the white sauce, stir it with a whisk while it cooks.*

SAGE-RUBBED SALMON

START TO FINISH: 20 MIN.
MAKES: 6 SERVINGS

- 2 **tablespoons minced fresh sage**
- 1 **teaspoon garlic powder**
- 1 **teaspoon kosher salt**
- 1 **teaspoon freshly ground pepper**
- 1 **skin-on salmon fillet (1½ pounds)**
- 2 **tablespoons olive oil**

1. Preheat oven to 375°. Mix the first four ingredients; rub onto flesh side of salmon. Cut into six portions.
2. In a large cast-iron skillet, heat oil over medium heat. Add salmon, skin side down; cook 5 minutes. Transfer skillet to oven; bake just until fish flakes easily with a fork, about 10 minutes.

If you've always thought of sage with turkey, try it with salmon for a little taste of heaven. We serve this with rice, salad and sauteed green beans.

—**NICOLE RASKOPF** BEACON, NY

SMOKIN'-PHILLED CHICKEN BREASTS

Combine cream cheese filling, crunchy coating and smoky heat from chipotle peppers in adobo sauce to seriously up your chicken dinner game.

—CAROLYN KUMPE EL DORADO, CA

PREP: 30 MIN. • **BAKE:** 15 MIN.
MAKES: 4 SERVINGS

- 1 package (8 ounces) cream cheese, softened
- ½ cup finely chopped fully cooked smoked ham
- 2 green onions, chopped
- 1 tablespoon minced chipotle pepper in adobo sauce
- ½ teaspoon salt
- ½ teaspoon smoked paprika
- 4 boneless skinless chicken breast halves (6 ounces each)
- ⅓ cup all-purpose flour
- 1 large egg, beaten
- 1 cup panko (Japanese) bread crumbs
- ¼ cup canola oil

1. Preheat oven to 400°. In a small bowl, combine the first six ingredients; set aside. Cut a pocket in the thickest part of each chicken breast; fill with the cream cheese mixture. Secure with toothpicks.

2. Place the flour, egg and bread crumbs in three separate shallow bowls. Coat each chicken breast with flour, then dip in egg mixture and coat with crumbs.

3. In a cast-iron or other ovenproof skillet, brown the chicken in oil over medium heat; transfer the skillet to the oven. Bake, uncovered, until a thermometer reads 170°, 15-20 minutes. Discard toothpicks before serving.

UPSIDE-DOWN MEAT PIE

This recipe, which my sister gave me more than 30 years ago, is perfect whenever friends drop by—it mixes up in a jiffy, yet it's substantial and satisfying.

—CORA DOWLING TOLEDO, OH

PREP: 25 MIN. • **BAKE:** 20 MIN.
MAKES: 4 SERVINGS

- 1 **pound ground beef**
- ½ **cup chopped onion**
- ½ **teaspoon salt**
- 1 **can (15 ounces) tomato sauce**

BAKING POWDER BISCUITS

- 1 **cup all-purpose flour**
- 2 **teaspoons baking powder**
- 1 **teaspoon celery salt**
- 1 **teaspoon paprika**
- ½ **teaspoon salt**
- ¼ **teaspoon pepper**
- 3 **tablespoons butter**
- ½ **cup milk**

1. Preheat oven to 475°. In a large ovenproof skillet, cook ground beef and onion over medium heat until the beef is browned and onion is tender; drain. Add salt and tomato sauce; simmer for 10-15 minutes.

2. Meanwhile, combine flour, baking powder, celery salt, paprika, salt and pepper in a bowl. Cut in the butter until the mixture resembles coarse meal. Add the milk and stir until a soft dough forms. Drop it by tablespoonfuls onto the meat mixture.

3. Bake, uncovered, for 20 minutes or until the biscuits are golden.

BREADS
&SIDES

BUTTERNUT SQUASH ROLLS

With their cheery yellow color and delicious aroma, these appealing rolls will brighten any buffet table. I've found the recipe is a great way to use garden-fresh squash.

—BERNICE MORRIS MARSHFIELD, MO

PREP: 30 MIN. + RISING • **BAKE:** 20 MIN.
MAKES: 2 DOZEN

- 1 package (¼ ounce) active dry yeast
- 1 cup warm whole milk (110° to 115°)
- ¼ cup warm water (110° to 115°)
- 3 tablespoons butter, softened
- 2 teaspoons salt
- ½ cup sugar
- 1 cup mashed cooked butternut squash
- 5 to 5½ cups all-purpose flour, divided

1. In a large bowl, dissolve yeast in milk and water. Add the butter, salt, sugar, squash and 3 cups flour; beat until smooth. Add enough remaining flour to form a soft dough.

2. Turn onto a floured surface; knead until smooth and elastic, 6-8 minutes. Place in a greased bowl, turning once to grease top. Cover and let rise in a warm place until doubled, about 1 hour.

3. Punch dough down. Form into rolls; place in two greased 10-in. cast-iron skillets or 9-in. round baking pans. Cover and let rise until doubled, about 30 minutes.

4. Bake at 375° for 20-25 minutes or until golden brown.

WONDERFUL ENGLISH MUFFINS

When I was growing up on a farm, my mom always seemed to be making homemade bread...nothing tasted so good! Now I like to make these simple yet delicious muffins for my own family. I love that they're made in a skillet.

—LINDA RASMUSSEN TWIN FALLS, ID

PREP: 30 MIN. + RISING • **COOK:** 25 MIN.
MAKES: 12-16 MUFFINS

- 1 **cup milk**
- ¼ **cup butter, cubed**
- 2 **tablespoons sugar**
- 1 **teaspoon salt**
- 2 **packages (¼ ounce each) active dry yeast**
- 1 **cup warm water (110° to 115°)**
- 2 **cups all-purpose flour**
- 3 **to 3½ cups whole wheat flour**
- 1 **tablespoon sesame seeds**
- 1 **tablespoon poppy seeds**
  Cornmeal

1. Scald milk in a saucepan; add butter, sugar and salt. Stir until butter melts; cool to lukewarm. In a small bowl, dissolve yeast in warm water; add to milk mixture. Stir in all-purpose flour and 1 cup whole wheat flour until smooth. Add sesame seeds, poppy seeds and enough remaining whole wheat flour to make a soft dough.

2. Turn onto a floured surface; knead until smooth and elastic, about 8-10 minutes. Place in a greased bowl, turning once to grease top. Cover and let rise until doubled, about 1 hour.

3. Punch dough down. Roll to ⅓-in. thickness on a cornmeal-covered surface. Cut into circles with a 3½-in. or 4-in. cutter; cover with a towel and let rise until nearly doubled, about 30 minutes.

4. Place muffins, cornmeal side down, in a greased skillet; cook over medium-low heat for 12-14 minutes or until bottoms are browned. Turn and cook about 12-14 minutes or until browned. Cool on wire racks; split muffins and toast to serve.

CALZONE ROLLS

PREP: 20 MIN. + RISING • **BAKE:** 20 MIN.
MAKES: 2 DOZEN

1⅔ cups water (**70° to 80°**)
2 tablespoons nonfat dry milk powder
2 tablespoons sugar
2 tablespoons shortening
1¼ teaspoons salt
4½ cups all-purpose flour
2¼ teaspoons active dry yeast
½ cup chopped onion
½ cup sliced fresh mushrooms
½ cup chopped green pepper
½ cup chopped sweet red pepper
1 tablespoon olive oil
⅓ cup pizza sauce
½ cup diced pepperoni
1 cup shredded pizza cheese blend
¼ cup chopped ripe olives
2 tablespoons grated Parmesan cheese

1. In bread machine pan, place the first seven ingredients in order suggested by manufacturer. Select dough setting (check dough after 5 minutes of mixing; add 1 to 2 tablespoons of water or flour if needed).

2. In a small skillet, saute the onion, mushrooms and peppers in oil until tender; cool. When bread machine cycle is completed, turn dough onto a lightly floured surface; divide in half. Let rest for 5 minutes.

3. Roll each portion of dough into a 16x10-in. rectangle; spread with pizza sauce. Top with the onion mixture, pepperoni, pizza cheese and olives. Roll up each rectangle jelly-roll style, starting with a long side; pinch seam to seal. Cut each into 12 slices (discard end pieces).

4. Place slices cut side down in two 10-in. cast-iron skillets or two greased 9-in. round baking pans. Sprinkle with Parmesan cheese. Cover and let rise until doubled, about 30 minutes.

5. Bake at 375° for 20-30 minutes or until golden brown. Serve warm.

Bite into big pizza flavor with these addictive rolls. The recipe makes two pans so there's always plenty to go around.
—**BARB DOWNIE** PETERBOROUGH, ON

HERB BREAD

My grandmother, aunts and mom were all good cooks, and each had her own specialty when it came to bread, but Mom's herb bread was my favorite. The flavors always remind me of cornbread stuffing!

—SHIRLEY SMITH YORBA LINDA, CA

PREP: 10 MIN. • **BAKE:** 35 MIN.
MAKES: 10 SERVINGS

- 1½ cups all-purpose flour
- 2 tablespoons sugar
- 4 teaspoons baking powder
- 1½ teaspoons salt
- 1 teaspoon rubbed sage
- 1 teaspoon dried thyme
- 1½ cups yellow cornmeal
- 1½ cups chopped celery
- 1 cup chopped onion
- 1 jar (2 ounces) chopped pimientos, drained
- 3 large eggs, beaten
- 1½ cups fat-free milk
- ⅓ cup vegetable oil

In a large bowl, combine the flour, sugar, baking powder, salt, sage and thyme. Combine cornmeal, celery, onion and pimientos; add to dry ingredients and mix well. Add eggs, milk and oil; stir just until moistened. Pour into a greased 10- or 11-in. ovenproof skillet. Bake at 400° for 35-45 minutes or until the bread tests done. Serve warm.

RAINBOW HASH

To get my family to eat outside their comfort zone, I use lots of color. This quick and easy side dish combines sweet potato, carrot, purple potato and kale.
—**COURTNEY STULTZ** WEIR, KS

START TO FINISH: 30 MIN
MAKES: 2 SERVINGS

- 2 tablespoons olive or coconut oil
- 1 medium sweet potato, peeled and cubed
- 1 medium purple potato, peeled and cubed
- 1 large carrot, peeled and cubed
- ½ teaspoon dried oregano
- ½ teaspoon dried basil
- ½ teaspoon sea salt
- ½ teaspoon pepper
- 2 cups fresh kale or spinach, coarsely chopped
- 1 small garlic clove, minced

In a large skillet, heat oil over medium heat. Cook and stir potatoes, carrot and seasonings until vegetables are tender, about 10-12 minutes. Add kale and garlic; continue cooking until vegetables are lightly browned and kale is tender, 2-4 minutes.

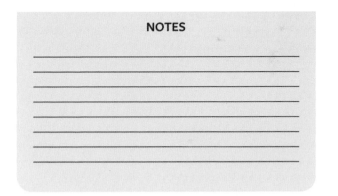

NOTES

HELPFUL HINT

Before using cornmeal in any recipe, make sure it's fresh. It should have a slightly sweet smell. Rancid cornmeal will smell stale and a bit musty.

GOLDEN SWEET ONION BREAD

Serve this hearty onion bread with generous scoops of cranberry butter.

—TASTE OF HOME TEST KITCHEN

PREP: 35 MIN.
BAKE: 20 MIN. + STANDING
MAKES: 8 SERVINGS

- 2 tablespoons butter
- 1 large sweet onion, halved and thinly sliced
- 4 teaspoons chopped seeded jalapeno pepper
- ½ teaspoon chili powder, divided
- 2 tablespoons brown sugar, divided
- 1½ cups all-purpose flour
- 1 cup yellow cornmeal
- 3 tablespoons sugar
- 2 teaspoons baking powder
- ½ teaspoon kosher salt
- ½ teaspoon baking soda
- 1¼ cups buttermilk
- 2 large eggs, lightly beaten
- ¼ cup butter, melted
- ¾ cup shredded cheddar cheese
- 1 can (4 ounces) chopped green chilies

CRANBERRY BUTTER
- ½ cup whole-berry cranberry sauce
- ½ teaspoon grated lime peel
- ½ cup butter, softened

1. In a 10-in. cast-iron skillet, melt 2 tablespoons butter; tilt to coat bottom and sides. Add the onion, jalapeno and ¼ teaspoon chili powder; cook over medium-low heat until onion is lightly browned and tender. Stir in 1 tablespoon brown sugar until dissolved; set aside.

2. In a large bowl, combine flour, cornmeal, sugar, baking powder, salt, baking soda, and remaining chili powder and brown sugar. In a small bowl, whisk the buttermilk, eggs and melted butter. Stir into dry ingredients just until moistened. Fold in cheese and chilies.

3. Pour over onion mixture in skillet. Bake at 425° for 20-25 minutes or until golden brown. Meanwhile, in a small saucepan, cook cranberry sauce and lime peel over low heat until heated through. Cool completely.

4. Let onion bread stand for 10 minutes. Invert onion bread onto a serving platter; cut into wedges. Pour cranberry mixture over softened butter; serve with warm onion bread.

NOTE *Wear disposable gloves when cutting hot peppers; the oils can burn skin. Avoid touching your face.*

HOMEY MAC & CHEESE

I also call this "My Grandson's Mac & Cheese." I've been privileged to make his favorite casserole for him for over 20 years. He particularly enjoyed it whenever he was on a leave from the military.

—ALICE BEARDSELL OSPREY, FL

PREP: 20 MIN. • **BAKE:** 25 MIN.
MAKES: 8 SERVINGS

- 2½ cups uncooked elbow macaroni
- ¼ cup butter, cubed
- ¼ cup all-purpose flour
- ½ teaspoon salt
- ¼ teaspoon pepper
- 3 cups 2% milk
- 5 cups shredded sharp cheddar cheese, divided
- 2 tablespoons Worcestershire sauce
- ½ teaspoon paprika

1. Preheat oven to 350°. Cook macaroni according to package directions for al dente.

2. Meanwhile, in a large saucepan, heat butter over medium heat. Stir in flour, salt and pepper until smooth; gradually whisk in milk. Bring to a boil, stirring constantly; cook and stir 2-3 minutes or until thickened.

3. Reduce heat. Stir in 3 cups cheese and Worcestershire sauce until cheese is melted.

4. Drain macaroni; stir into sauce. Transfer to a greased 10-in. ovenproof skillet. Bake, uncovered, 20 minutes. Top with remaining cheese; sprinkle with paprika. Bake until bubbly and cheese is melted, 5-10 minutes.

FRY BREAD

After enjoying Navajo tacos at a restaurant, I went home and created my own recipe for fry bread. Our daughter's friend, a Navajo Indian, helped me improve it and this is the tasty result. I've served this often—both at home and on the ranch where I work. Everyone loves it!

—THELMA TYLER DRAGOON, AZ

PREP: 20 MIN. • **COOK:** 15 MIN.
MAKES: 12 FRY BREADS

- 2 cups unbleached flour
- ½ teaspoon salt
- ½ cup nonfat dry milk powder
- 3 teaspoons baking powder
- 4½ teaspoons shortening
- ⅔ to ¾ cup water
  Oil for deep-fat frying
  Butter, honey and lemon juice, optional

1. Combine flour, dry milk powder, baking powder and salt; cut in shortening until crumbly. Add water gradually, mixing to form a firm ball. Divide dough; shape into 12 balls. Let stand, covered, for 10 minutes. Roll each ball into a 6-in. circle. With a sharp knife, cut a ½-in.-diameter hole in center of each.

2. In a large cast-iron skillet, heat oil over medium-high heat. Fry dough circles, one at a time, until puffed and golden, about 1 minute on each side. Drain on paper towels; if desired, serve warm with butter, honey and fresh lemon juice.

MEAT & PEPPER CORNBREAD

It suits me to be able to brown and bake this hearty cornbread in the same cast-iron skillet. Serve it alongside soup, stew or barbecued meats or on its own.

—RITA CARLSON IDAHO FALLS, ID

PREP: 15 MIN. • **BAKE:** 20 MIN.
MAKES: 4-6 SERVINGS

- 1 **pound ground beef**
- 1 **cup chopped green pepper**
- 1 **cup chopped onion**
- 2 **cans (8 ounces each) tomato sauce**
- 1½ **teaspoons chili powder**
- ½ **teaspoon salt**
- ¼ **teaspoon pepper**
- 1 **cup all-purpose flour**
- ¾ **cup cornmeal**
- ¼ **cup sugar**
- 1 **tablespoon baking powder**
- ½ **teaspoon salt**
- 1 **large egg, beaten**
- 1 **cup milk**
- ¼ **cup canola oil**

1. In a 10-in. cast-iron or other ovenproof skillet, lightly brown ground beef, green pepper and onion; drain. Add tomato sauce, chili powder, salt and pepper; simmer 10-15 minutes.
2. Meanwhile, combine dry ingredients. Combine egg, milk and oil; stir into dry ingredients just until moistened. Pour over beef mixture.
3. Bake at 400° for 20-25 minutes or until golden. Serve in skillet. Or cool briefly, then run a knife around edge of skillet and invert on a serving plate; cut into wedges.

AMISH ONION CAKE

This rich, moist bread with an onion-poppy seed topping is a wonderful break from your everyday bread routine. You can serve it with any meat, and it's a nice accompaniment to an entree salad or thick soup.

—MITZI SENTIFF ANNAPOLIS, MD

PREP: 25 MIN. • **BAKE:** 35 MIN.
MAKES: 10-12 SERVINGS

- 3 to 4 medium onions, chopped
- 2 cups cold butter, divided
- 1 tablespoon poppy seeds
- 1½ teaspoons salt
- 1½ teaspoons paprika
- 1 teaspoon coarsely ground pepper
- 4 cups all-purpose flour
- ½ cup cornstarch
- 1 tablespoon baking powder
- 1 tablespoon sugar
- 1 tablespoon brown sugar
- 5 large eggs
- ¾ cup 2% milk
- ¾ cup sour cream

1. In a large skillet, cook onions in ½ cup butter over low heat for 10 minutes. Stir in the poppy seeds, salt, paprika and pepper; cook until golden brown, stirring occasionally. Remove from the heat; set aside.

2. In a large bowl, combine the flour, cornstarch, baking powder and sugars. Cut in 1¼ cups butter until mixture resembles coarse crumbs. Melt the remaining butter. In a small bowl, whisk the eggs, milk, sour cream and melted butter. Make a well in dry ingredients; stir in egg mixture just until moistened.

3. Spread into a greased 10-in. cast-iron skillet or 10-in. springform pan. Spoon onion mixture over the dough. (If using a springform pan, place pan on a baking sheet.) Bake at 350° for 35-40 minutes or until a toothpick inserted near the center comes out clean. Serve warm.

HELPFUL HINT

Be sure not to overmix cornbread batter. To avoid overmixing, stir the batter by hand just until moistened. Lumps in the batter are actually desired.

JALAPENO BUTTERMILK CORNBREAD

If you're from the South, you have to have a good corn bread recipe. Here's a lightened-up version of my mom's traditional cornbread.

—DEBI MITCHELL FLOWER MOUND, TX

PREP: 15 MIN. • **BAKE:** 20 MIN.
MAKES: 8 SERVINGS

- 1 **cup self-rising flour**
- 1 **cup yellow cornmeal**
- 1 **cup buttermilk**
- ¼ **cup egg substitute**
- 3 **tablespoon canola oil, divided**
- 2 **tablespoons honey**
- 1 **tablespoon reduced-fat mayonnaise**
- ¼ **cup fresh or frozen corn, thawed**
- 3 **tablespoons shredded reduced-fat cheddar cheese**
- 3 **tablespoons finely chopped sweet red pepper**
- ½ **to 1 jalapeno pepper, seeded and finely chopped**

1. Preheat oven to 425°. In a large bowl, whisk flour and cornmeal. In another bowl, whisk buttermilk, egg substitute, 2 tablespoons oil, honey and mayonnaise. Pour remaining oil into an 8-in. ovenproof skillet; place skillet in oven 4 minutes.

2. Meanwhile, add buttermilk mixture to flour mixture; stir just until moistened. Fold in corn, cheese and peppers.

3. Carefully tilt and rotate skillet to coat bottom with oil; add batter. Bake 20-25 minutes or until a toothpick inserted in center comes out clean. Serve warm.

NOTE *As a substitute for 1 cup of self-rising flour, place 1½ teaspoons baking powder and ½ teaspoon salt in a measuring cup. Add all-purpose flour to measure 1 cup. Wear disposable gloves when cutting hot peppers; the oils can burn skin. Avoid touching your face.*

ORANGE-GLAZED CARROTS, ONIONS & RADISHES

Carrots and radishes give color and crunch to this sweet, spicy side. We never have leftovers. If you make it ahead, reheat and add the walnuts before serving.

—THOMAS FAGLON SOMERSET, NJ

PREP: 15 MIN. • **COOK:** 20 MIN.
MAKES: 8 SERVINGS

- 1 **pound fresh pearl onions**
- ¼ **cup butter, cubed**
- 2 **pounds medium carrots, thinly sliced**
- 12 **radishes, thinly sliced**
- ½ **cup dark brown sugar**
- 4 **teaspoons grated orange peel**
- ½ **cup orange juice**
- 1 **cup chopped walnuts, toasted**

1. In a large saucepan, bring 4 cups water to a boil. Add pearl onions; boil 3 minutes. Drain and rinse with cold water. Peel.
2. In a large skillet, heat butter over medium heat. Add carrots, pearl onions, radishes, brown sugar, orange peel and juice; cook, covered, 10-15 minutes or until vegetables are tender, stirring occasionally. Cook, uncovered, 5-7 minutes longer or until slightly thickened. Sprinkle with walnuts.
NOTE *To toast nuts, bake in a shallow pan in a 350° oven for 5-10 minutes or cook in a skillet over low heat until lightly browned, stirring occasionally.*

SPICED APPLE BREAD

There's just nothing better than a big piece of cornbread to go with a supper of fried chicken, chops or baked ham! I've sweetened things up with a little apple and spice, and everyone raves over the tender, moist and delicious results.

—KELLY WILLIAMS FORKED RIVER, NJ

PREP: 15 MIN. • **BAKE:** 40 MIN.
MAKES: 12 SERVINGS

- 2 **cups all-purpose flour**
- 2 **cups yellow cornmeal**
- 1 **tablespoon baking powder**
- 1 **teaspoon salt**
- ½ **teaspoon ground cinnamon**
- ½ **teaspoon pumpkin pie spice**
- ½ **cup butter, softened**
- 1½ **cups sugar**
- ½ **teaspoon vanilla extract**
- 4 **large eggs**
- 2 **cups water**
- 1 **cup shredded peeled apple**

1. Preheat oven to 400°. Whisk together first six ingredients. In a large bowl, beat butter and sugar until blended. Add vanilla and eggs, one at a time, beating well after each. Stir in flour mixture alternately with water, adding water slowly (mixture may appear slightly curdled). Stir in apple.

2. Transfer to a greased 10-in. cast-iron skillet (pan will be very full). Bake on a lower oven rack until a toothpick inserted in center comes out clean, 40-50 minutes. Serve cornbread warm.

SKILLET ZUCCHINI & SAUSAGE

START TO FINISH: 30 MIN.
MAKES: 8-10 SERVINGS

- 2 tablespoons vegetable oil
- ½ pound fully cooked smoked Polish sausage, cut into ½-inch diagonal slices
- 1 cup chopped onion
- 1 cup sliced celery
- ½ cup chopped green pepper
- 1 garlic clove, minced
- ½ teaspoon dried oregano
- ½ teaspoon pepper
- 4 to 5 medium zucchini, sliced
- 4 to 5 medium tomatoes, coarsely chopped
  Herb seasoning blend to taste

Heat oil in a large skillet, lightly brown sausage. Add onion, celery, green pepper, garlic, oregano and pepper. Cook and stir until vegetables are almost tender. Add zucchini and tomatoes; cook and stir until zucchini is just tender. Sprinkle with seasoning blend.

I lived on the Oregon coast for 20 years, and during that time I had plenty of guests. I often turned to this dish when folks dropped by because it was easy to make, took little time to prepare and can be served as a side or a light entree. No matter how it's served, everyone seems to love it!

—**LABELLE DOSTER** VANCOUVER, WA

CAMPFIRE
READY

CREOLE CORNBREAD

Cornbread is a staple of Cajun and Creole cuisine. This is an old favorite that I found in the bottom of my recipe drawer, and I'm so glad I did! It's just wonderful.

—ENID HEBERT LAFAYETTE, LA

PREP: 15 MIN. • **BAKE:** 45 MIN.
MAKES: 12 SERVINGS

- 2 **cups cooked rice**
- 1 **cup yellow cornmeal**
- ½ **cup chopped onion**
- 1 **to 2 tablespoons seeded chopped jalapeno peppers**
- 1 **teaspoon salt**
- ½ **teaspoon baking soda**
- 2 **large eggs**
- 1 **cup whole milk**
- ¼ **cup canola oil**
- 1 **can (16½ ounces) cream-style corn**
- 3 **cups shredded cheddar cheese**
  Additional cornmeal

1. In a large bowl, combine rice, cornmeal, onion, peppers, salt and baking soda.

2. In another bowl, beat eggs, milk and oil. Add corn; mix well. Stir into rice mixture until blended. Fold in cheese. Sprinkle a well-greased 10-in. ovenproof skillet with cornmeal. Pour batter into skillet.

3. Bake at 350° for 45-50 minutes or until bread tests done. Cut into wedges and serve warm.

NOTE *Wear disposable gloves when cutting hot peppers; the oils can burn skin. Avoid touching your face.*

POTATO PAN ROLLS

My family loves these rolls, which is why they're requested often. They don't take long to make if you use quick-rise yeast.

—CONNIE STORCKMAN EVANSTON, WY

PREP: 15 MIN. + RISING • **BAKE:** 20 MIN.
MAKES: 16 ROLLS

4½ to 5 cups all-purpose flour
3 tablespoons sugar
2 packages (¼ ounce each) quick-rise yeast
1½ teaspoons salt
1¼ cups water
3 tablespoons butter
½ cup mashed potatoes (without added milk and butter)
Additional all-purpose flour

1. In a large bowl, combine 2 cups flour, sugar, yeast and salt. In a small saucepan, heat water and butter to 120°-130°. Add to dry ingredients; beat until smooth. Stir in mashed potatoes and enough remaining flour to form a soft dough.
2. Turn onto a floured surface; knead until smooth and elastic, about 6-8 minutes. Cover and let rest for 10 minutes. Divide into 16 pieces. Shape each into a ball. Place in two greased 8- or 9-in. round baking pans or ovenproof skillets. Cover and let rise in a warm place until doubled, about 30 minutes.
3. Preheat oven to 400°. Sprinkle tops of rolls with additional flour. Bake 18-22 minutes or until golden brown. Remove from pans to wire racks.

MUENSTER BREAD

PREP: 20 MIN. + RISING
BAKE: 45 MIN. + COOLING
MAKES: 1 LOAF (16 SLICES)

- 2 **packages (¼ ounce each) active dry yeast**
- 1 **cup warm milk (110° to 115°)**
- ½ **cup butter, softened**
- 2 **tablespoons sugar**
- 1 **teaspoon salt**
- 3¼ to 3¾ **cups all-purpose flour**
- 1 **large egg plus 1 large egg yolk**
- 4 **cups shredded Muenster cheese**
- 1 **large egg white, beaten**

1. In a large bowl, dissolve yeast in milk. Add the butter, sugar, salt and 2 cups flour; beat until smooth. Stir in enough remaining flour to form a soft dough.

2. Turn onto a floured surface; knead until smooth and elastic, about 6-8 minutes. Place in a greased bowl, turning once to grease top. Cover and let rise in a warm place until doubled, about 1 hour.

3. In a large bowl, beat egg and yolk; stir in cheese. Punch down dough; roll into a 16-in. circle.

4. Place in a greased 10-in. cast-iron skillet or 9-in. round baking pan, letting dough drape over the edges. Spoon the cheese mixture into center of dough. Gather dough up over filling in 1½-in. pleats. Gently squeeze pleats together at top and twist to make a top knot. Allow to rise 10-15 minutes.

5. Brush loaf with egg white. Bake at 375° for 40-45 minutes. Cool on a wire rack for 20 minutes. Serve bread warm.

My sister and I won blue ribbons with this bread many years ago. The recipe makes a beautiful, round golden loaf. With a layer of cheese peeking out of every slice, it's definitely a winner and worth the effort.

—MELANIE MERO IDA, MI

CRISPS, COBBLERS & MORE

CHERRY-PEACH DUMPLINGS

This sweet dessert is made from start to finish on your stovetop; there's no more convenient way to enjoy the delicious taste of fruit, even out of season.

—PATRICIA FRERK SYRACUSE, NY

PREP: 15 MIN. • **COOK:** 20 MIN.
MAKES: 6 SERVINGS

- 1 **can (21 ounces) cherry pie filling**
- ½ **cup water**
- 2 **tablespoons lemon juice**
- ½ **teaspoon ground cinnamon**
- ¼ **teaspoon ground cloves**
- 1 **can (15¼ ounces) sliced peaches, drained**
- 1 **large egg**
  Whole milk
- 1½ **cups biscuit/baking mix**
  Additional cinnamon and whipped cream, optional

1. In a 10-in. skillet, combine the first five ingredients. Add peaches; bring to a boil.

2. Place egg in a 1-cup measuring cup; add enough milk to equal ½ cup. Place biscuit mix in a bowl; stir in egg mixture with a fork just until moistened. Drop by six spoonfuls over top of boiling fruit.

3. Simmer, uncovered, for 10 minutes; cover and simmer 10 minutes longer or until a toothpick inserted into a dumpling comes out clean. Sprinkle with cinnamon if desired. Serve warm with whipped cream if desired.

MILK CAKE

This is a simple recipe—and you'll be able to use your well-seasoned cast-iron skillet to make it. The result of your effort is a light, airy cake.

—SUZANNE COLEMAN RABUN GAP, GA

PREP: 20 MIN. • **BAKE:** 30 MIN.
MAKES: 8 SERVINGS

- ½ cup whole milk
- ¾ cup all-purpose flour
- 1 teaspoon baking powder
- ¼ teaspoon salt
- 3 large eggs, room temperature
- 1 teaspoon vanilla extract
- 1 cup sugar

TOPPING

- ⅓ cup packed brown sugar
- ½ cup chopped pecans
- 2 tablespoons butter, softened
- 2 tablespoons whole milk
- 1 cup sweetened shredded coconut

1. Preheat oven to 350°. In a saucepan, scald the milk; set aside. Combine flour, baking powder and salt; set aside. In a bowl, beat eggs until thick and lemon-colored; stir in vanilla. Gradually add sugar, blending well. On low speed, alternately mix in milk and dry ingredients. Pour batter into a greased 10-in. cast-iron skillet.

2. Bake for 25-30 minutes or until the cake springs back when lightly touched. Remove the cake from the oven and preheat the broiler.

3. Combine all topping ingredients and sprinkle over cake. Broil 5 in. from the heat until topping bubbles and turns golden brown. Serve warm.

GRANDMA PRUIT'S VINEGAR PIE

This historic pie has been in our family for many generations and is always at all of the family get-togethers.
—**SUZETTE PRUIT** HOUSTON, TX

PREP: 40 MIN. • **BAKE:** 1 HOUR
MAKES: 8 SERVINGS

- 2 **cups sugar**
- 3 **tablespoons all-purpose flour**
- ¼ **to ½ teaspoon ground nutmeg**
  Pastry for double-crust pie (9 inches)
- ½ **cup butter, cubed**
- ⅔ **cup white vinegar**
- 1 **quart hot water**

1. Preheat oven to 450°. Whisk together the sugar, flour and nutmeg; set aside. On a lightly floured surface, roll one-third of the pie dough to a ⅛-in.-thick circle; cut into 2x1-in. strips. Layer a deep 12-in. enamel-coated cast-iron skillet or ovenproof casserole with half the dough strips; sprinkle with half the sugar mixture. Dot with half the butter. Repeat sugar and butter layers.

2. Roll the remaining two-thirds of the pie dough into a ⅛-in.-thick circle. Place over the filling, pressing against the sides of the skillet. Cut a slit in top. Add vinegar to hot water; slowly pour vinegar mixture through the slit in the crust. Liquid may bubble up through crust; this is normal. To catch spills, line an oven rack with foil.

3. Bake until crust is golden brown, about 1 hour. Cover the edge loosely with foil during the last 15-20 minutes if needed to prevent overbrowning. Remove foil. Cool on a wire rack.

PASTRY FOR DOUBLE-CRUST PIE (9 INCHES):
Combine 2½ cups all-purpose flour and ½ tsp. salt; cut in 1 cup cold butter until crumbly. Gradually add ⅓ to ⅔ cup ice water, tossing with a fork until dough holds together when pressed. Divide dough in two portions. Shape each portion into a disk; wrap in plastic wrap. Refrigerate 1 hour or overnight.

BLACK & BLUE BERRY GRUNT

If you are looking for something different than the usual cakes and fruit pies, try this old-fashioned dessert. It features a delicious combination of blackberries and blueberries with homemade dumplings on top.

—KELLY AKIN JOHNSONVILLE, NY

START TO FINISH: 30 MIN.
MAKES: 8 SERVINGS

- 2½ **cups fresh or frozen blackberries, thawed**
- 2½ **cups fresh or frozen blueberries, thawed**
- ¾ **cup sugar**
- ¼ **cup water**
- 1 **tablespoon lemon juice**
- ⅛ **teaspoon ground cinnamon**
- ⅛ **teaspoon pepper**

DUMPLINGS
- 1 **cup all-purpose flour**
- 2 **tablespoons sugar**
- 1 **teaspoon baking powder**
- ½ **teaspoon baking soda**
- ⅛ **teaspoon salt**
- 2 **tablespoons butter, melted**
- ½ **cup buttermilk**
- 1 **tablespoon cinnamon-sugar**
  Sweetened whipped cream, optional

1. In a large skillet, combine the first seven ingredients. Bring to a boil. Reduce heat; simmer, uncovered, for 5 minutes.

2. Meanwhile, in a large bowl, combine the first five dumpling ingredients. Add butter and buttermilk; stir just until moistened. Drop by tablespoonfuls onto the berry mixture. Sprinkle with cinnamon-sugar.

3. Cover tightly; simmer until a toothpick inserted in a dumpling comes out clean, 10-15 minutes. Serve warm; if desired, add sweetened whipped cream.

CINNAMON APPLE PAN BETTY

I found this recipe soon after I was married 47 years ago. You'll need just a few ingredients, which you probably have on hand. It's super quick to put together, too. It's a favorite of ours during fall and winter, when apples are at their best.

—SHIRLEY LEISTER WEST CHESTER, PA

START TO FINISH: 15 MIN.
MAKES: 2 SERVINGS

- 3 **medium apples, peeled and cubed**
- ½ **cup butter**
- 3 **cups cubed bread**
- ½ **cup sugar**
- ¾ **teaspoon ground cinnamon**

In a large skillet, saute apples in butter for 4-5 minutes or until tender. Add bread cubes. Stir together sugar and cinnamon; sprinkle over the apple mixture and toss to coat. Saute until bread is warmed.

NOTES

_____

_____

_____

_____

_____

_____

_____

_____

FUDGE BROWNIE PIE

PREP: 15 MIN. • **BAKE:** 25 MIN.
MAKES: 6 SERVINGS

- 1 **cup sugar**
- ½ **cup butter, melted**
- 2 **large eggs**
- 1 **teaspoon vanilla extract**
- ½ **cup all-purpose flour**
- ⅓ **cup baking cocoa**
- ¼ **teaspoon salt**
- ½ **cup chopped pecans**
  Whipped cream, optional
  Strawberries, optional

1. Preheat oven to 350°. In a large bowl, beat sugar and butter. Add eggs and vanilla; mix well. Add flour, cocoa and salt. Stir in nuts.

2. Pour into a greased ovenproof skilled or 9-in. pie pan. Bake for 25-30 minutes or until almost set. Serve with whipped cream and strawberries if desired.

Here's a fun and festive way to serve brownies. Family and friends will love topping their pieces with whipped cream and strawberries.

—JOHNNIE MCLEOD BASTROP, LA

SKILLET CHOCOLATE DUMPLINGS

Why bake when you can make an entire dessert on the stovetop? My family often requests these dumplings for birthdays and other special events.

—BECKY MAGEE CHANDLER, AZ

PREP: 20 MIN. • **COOK:** 20 MIN.
MAKES: 6-8 SERVINGS

¾ **cup packed brown sugar**
¼ **cup baking cocoa**
1 **tablespoon cornstarch**
   Dash salt
2 **cups water**
2 **tablespoons butter**

DUMPLINGS

1¼ **cups all-purpose flour**
2 **teaspoons baking powder**
½ **teaspoon salt**
½ **cup sugar**
2 **tablespoons baking cocoa**
3 **tablespoons butter**
1 **large egg, lightly beaten**
⅓ **cup milk**
1 **teaspoon vanilla extract**
   Whipped cream or ice cream

1. For sauce, combine brown sugar, cocoa, cornstarch and salt in a large cast-iron or other heavy, ovenproof skillet. Stir in the water; cook, stirring constantly, until mixture begins to boil and thicken slightly. Add butter; mix well. Remove from heat.

2. For dumplings, sift together the flour, baking powder, salt, sugar and cocoa. Cut in the butter until the mixture resembles a fine meal. Combine the egg, milk and vanilla; blend gradually into the flour mixture.

3. Return the skillet to the heat; bring the sauce to a boil. Drop dumplings by tablespoons into sauce. Reduce heat to low; cover and simmer until just set, about 20 minutes. Serve warm with whipped cream or ice cream.

BANANAS FOSTER SUNDAES

I have such wonderful memories of eating Bananas Foster in New Orleans—but as a dietitian, I wanted to find a healthier version. I combined the best of two recipes and made my own tweaks to create this Southern treat.

—LISA VARNER EL PASO, TX

START TO FINISH: 15 MIN.
MAKES: 6 SERVINGS

- 1 **tablespoon butter**
- 3 **tablespoons brown sugar**
- 1 **tablespoon orange juice**
- ¼ **teaspoon ground cinnamon**
- ¼ **teaspoon ground nutmeg**
- 3 **large firm bananas, sliced**
- 2 **tablespoons chopped pecans, toasted**
- ½ **teaspoon rum extract**
- 3 **cups reduced-fat vanilla ice cream**

1. In an 8- or 9-in. cast-iron or other ovenproof skillet, melt butter over medium-low heat. Stir in the brown sugar, orange juice, cinnamon and nutmeg until blended. Add bananas and pecans; cook until the bananas are glazed and slightly softened, 2-3 minutes, stirring gently.

2. Remove from the heat; stir in extract. Serve with ice cream.

NOTE *To toast nuts, bake in a shallow pan in a 350° oven for 5-10 minutes or cook in a skillet over low heat until lightly browned, stirring occasionally.*

HELPFUL HINT

Use either light or dark brown sugar to suit your taste. Light brown has less molasses flavor and is more delicate. Dark brown tastes more "old-fashioned" and has a stronger molasses flavor.

SKILLET BLUEBERRY SLUMP

My mother-in-law made a slump of wild blueberries with dumplings and served it warm with a pitcher of farm cream. We've been eating slump for nearly 60 years!
—**ELEANORE EBELING** BREWSTER, MN

PREP: 25 MIN. • **BAKE:** 20 MIN.
MAKES: 6 SERVINGS

- 4 **cups fresh or frozen blueberries**
- ½ **cup sugar**
- ½ **cup water**
- 1 **teaspoon grated lemon peel**
- 1 **tablespoon lemon juice**
- 1 **cup all-purpose flour**
- 2 **tablespoons sugar**
- 2 **teaspoons baking powder**
- ½ **teaspoon salt**
- 1 **tablespoon butter**
- ½ **cup 2% milk**
  Vanilla ice cream

1. Preheat the oven to 400°. In a 10-in. ovenproof skillet, combine the first five ingredients; bring to boil. Reduce heat; simmer, uncovered, for 9-11 minutes or until slightly thickened, stirring the mixture occasionally.

2. Meanwhile, in a small bowl, whisk flour, sugar, baking powder and salt. Cut in the butter until the mixture resembles coarse crumbs. Add milk; stir just until moistened.

3. Drop batter in six portions on top of the simmering blueberry mixture. Transfer to the oven. Bake, uncovered, 17-20 minutes or until the dumplings are golden brown. Serve warm with ice cream.

NOTES

CRANBERRY PECAN UPSIDE-DOWN CAKE

At our house, cranberries rate as a favorite. This dessert is one that I made for the first time just last fall. It started out as a pineapple upside-down cake—I simply changed a few things around! Because it keeps well and travels well, it is great for taking to church dinners.

—DORIS HEATH FRANKLIN, NC

PREP: 20 MIN. • **BAKE:** 30 MIN.
MAKES: 10 SERVINGS

- ½ **cup butter, cubed**
- 2 **cups sugar, divided**
- 1 **can (14 ounces) whole-berry cranberry sauce**
- ½ **cup coarsely chopped pecans**
- 3 **large eggs, separated**
- ⅓ **cup orange juice**
- 1 **cup all-purpose flour**
- 1 **teaspoon baking powder**
- ¼ **teaspoon salt**

1. Preheat the oven to 375°. Melt the butter in a 10-in. cast-iron skillet over medium heat. Add 1 cup of the sugar; cook and stir for 3 minutes. Remove from heat. Spoon cranberry sauce over the butter mixture; sprinkle pecans over all. Set aside.

2. In a bowl, beat egg yolks until foamy. Gradually add the remaining sugar; beat well. Blend in orange juice. Combine flour, baking powder and salt; add to the egg mixture. Beat egg whites until stiff; fold into batter.

3. Carefully spoon the batter over topping in skillet. Bake about 30 minutes or until cake tests done. Cool 5 minutes in the skillet, then invert onto a large serving plate. Serve warm.

DATE PUDDING COBBLER

There were eight children in the family when I was growing up, and all of us enjoyed this cobbler. I now serve it for everyday and special occasions alike.

—CAROLYN MILLER GUYS MILLS, PA

PREP: 15 MIN. • **BAKE:** 25 MIN.
MAKES: 6-8 SERVINGS

- 1 **cup all-purpose flour**
- 1½ **cups packed brown sugar, divided**
- 2 **teaspoons baking powder**
- 1 **tablespoon cold butter**
- ½ **cup milk**
- ¾ **cup chopped dates**
- ¾ **cup chopped walnuts**
- 1 **cup water**
  Whipped cream and ground cinnamon, optional

1. Preheat oven to 350°. In a large bowl, combine the flour, ½ cup of the brown sugar and the baking powder. Cut in the butter until crumbly. Gradually add the milk, dates and walnuts.
2. In a large saucepan, combine water and the remaining brown sugar; bring to a boil. Remove from the heat; add the date mixture and mix well.
3. Transfer to a greased 10-in. cast-iron skillet or 8-in. square baking pan. Bake for 25-30 minutes or until top is golden brown and fruit is tender. Serve warm.

NOTES

PEAR-PECAN CRISP WITH LEMON SAUCE

PREP: 30 MIN. • **BAKE:** 30 MIN.
MAKES: 6 SERVINGS

- 5 **cups sliced peeled ripe pears (about 5 medium)**
- 1 **tablespoon sugar**
- ⅔ **cup old-fashioned oats**
- ⅓ **cup all-purpose flour**
- ⅓ **cup packed brown sugar**
- ¼ **teaspoon ground cinnamon**
- ¼ **cup cold butter**
- ⅓ **cup chopped pecans**

SAUCE

- ¼ **cup sugar**
- 2 **teaspoons cornstarch**
- ½ **cup water**
- 1 **large egg yolk, beaten**
- 1 **tablespoon butter**
- 1 **tablespoon lemon juice**
- ¼ **teaspoon grated lemon peel**

1. Preheat the oven to 350°. Place pears in a greased 8-in. cast-iron skillet or 8-in. square baking dish; sprinkle with sugar. In a small bowl, combine oats, flour, brown sugar and cinnamon. Cut in the butter until the mixture resembles coarse crumbs; stir in the pecans. Sprinkle over pears. Bake 30-35 minutes or until bubbly.

2. Meanwhile, in a small saucepan, combine the sugar, cornstarch and water. Cook and stir over medium-high heat until mix is thickened and bubbly. Reduce heat; cook and stir 2 minutes longer.

3. Remove from the heat. Stir a small amount of the hot mixture into the egg yolk; return all to the pan, stirring constantly. Bring to a gentle boil; cook and stir 2 minutes longer. Remove from the heat; stir in the butter, lemon juice and peel. Serve with warm pear crisp.

Pear-adise on a plate is a great way to describe this fruity crisp! A lovely lemon custard sauce tops tender pears and crunchy topping.

—LISA VARNER EL PASO, TX

HELPFUL HINT

Old-fashioned oats and quick-cooking oats can be interchanged in baked goods, but old-fashioned oats add more texture.

GINGER MANGO GRUNT

These tender dumplings in a chunky fruit sauce are loaded with vitamins C and A, helpful in nourishing and protecting skin.

Roxanne Chan—Albany, CA

—ROXANNE CHAN ALBANY, CA

PREP: 25 MIN. • **COOK:** 20 MIN.
MAKES: 8 SERVINGS

- ½ cup all-purpose flour
- 3 tablespoons yellow cornmeal
- 4½ teaspoons sugar
- 1 teaspoon baking powder
- ¼ teaspoon ground ginger
- ⅛ teaspoon salt
- 2 tablespoons cold butter
- 3 tablespoons egg substitute
- ¾ cup mango nectar, divided
- 1 jar (20 ounces) refrigerated mango slices, drained
- ½ cup reduced-sugar orange marmalade
- 1 tablespoon lemon juice
- ½ cup golden raisins
- ¼ cup chopped crystallized ginger
- ¼ cup sliced almonds
  Low-fat frozen yogurt, optional

1. In a small bowl, combine the first six ingredients. Cut in the butter until the mixture resembles coarse crumbs. Combine egg substitute and ¼ cup of the nectar; stir into the flour mixture just until moistened.

2. Coarsely chop mango slices; combine with marmalade, lemon juice and the remaining nectar.

3. Transfer to an 8-in. cast-iron or other ovenproof skillet; stir in raisins. Bring to a boil. Drop flour mixture in eight mounds onto the simmering mango mixture. Reduce heat; cover and simmer for 12-15 minutes or until a toothpick inserted in a dumpling comes out clean (do not lift the cover while simmering). Sprinkle with ginger and almonds; if desired, serve with frozen yogurt.

SPICED PINEAPPLE UPSIDE-DOWN CAKE

Upside-down cakes, which have been around since the 1800s, used to be called skillet cakes because they were cooked in cast-iron skillets on the stovetop.

—JENNIFER SERGESKETTER
NEWBURGH, IN

PREP: 15 MIN. • **BAKE:** 40 MIN.
MAKES: 12 SERVINGS

- 1⅓ cups butter, softened, divided
- 1 cup packed brown sugar
- 1 can (20 ounces) pineapple slices, drained
- 10 to 12 maraschino cherries
- ½ cup chopped pecans
- 1½ cups sugar
- 2 large eggs
- 1 teaspoon vanilla extract
- 2 cups all-purpose flour
- 2 teaspoons baking powder
- ½ teaspoon baking soda
- ½ teaspoon salt
- ½ teaspoon ground cinnamon
- ½ teaspoon ground nutmeg
- 1 cup buttermilk

1. Preheat the oven to 350°. In a saucepan, melt ⅔ cup of the butter; stir in brown sugar. Spread into the bottom of an ungreased heavy 12-in skillet or a 13x9-in. baking pan. Arrange the pineapple slices in a single layer over the sugar mixture; place a cherry in the center of each slice. Sprinkle with pecans and set aside.

2. In a large bowl, cream sugar and the remaining butter until light and fluffy. Add the eggs, one at a time, beating well after each addition. Beat in vanilla. Combine the flour, baking powder, baking soda, salt, cinnamon and nutmeg; add alternately to the batter with the buttermilk, beating well after each addition.

3. Carefully pour the batter over the pineapple. Bake for 40 minutes for a skillet (50-60 minutes for baking pan) or until a toothpick inserted near the center comes out clean. Immediately invert onto a serving platter. Serve warm.

GINGERED CHERRY PEAR COBBLER

This fruit cobbler is warm, sweet and filling—comfort food perfected! It's great for those crisp and cool autumn days, and is best when served warm.

—TASTE OF HOME TEST KITCHEN

PREP: 25 MIN. • **BAKE:** 55 MIN.
MAKES: 8 SERVINGS

- **4 cups chopped peeled fresh pears**
- **½ cup dried cherries**
- **¼ cup packed brown sugar**
- **2 tablespoons finely chopped crystallized ginger**
- **1 tablespoon all-purpose flour**
- **3 tablespoons butter**

TOPPING

- **¼ cup sugar**
- **2 tablespoons finely chopped crystallized ginger**
- **1 cup all-purpose flour**
- **1½ teaspoons baking powder**
- **⅛ teaspoon baking soda**
- **¼ teaspoon salt**
- **5 tablespoons cold butter, cubed**
- **½ cup buttermilk**

1. Preheat the oven to 350°. In a large bowl, combine the first five ingredients; transfer to a greased 12-in. cast-iron skillet or to a 2-qt. baking dish. Heat butter in a small saucepan over medium heat for 7 minutes or until golden brown; pour over the pear mixture. Cover and bake for 20-25 minutes or until bubbly.

2. In a food processor, combine the sugar and ginger; cover and process until finely chopped. Add the flour, baking powder, baking soda and salt; cover and process for 3 seconds or until blended. Add the butter; process until mixture resembles coarse crumbs. Add buttermilk and pulse just until a soft dough forms. Drop by tablespoonfuls over warm pear mixture.

3. Bake it, uncovered, for 35-40 minutes or until topping is golden brown. Serve warm.

GINGERED CRANBERRY-PEAR COBBLER *Substitute dried cranberries for the cherries.*

GINGERED RAISIN-PEAR COBBLER *Substitute golden raisins for the cherries.*

CARAMEL DUMPLINGS

My family just loves these tender dumplings in a sweet, rich sauce. I love them because they turn out wonderful every time I make them...which is a lot!

—FAYE JOHNSON CONNERSVILLE, IN

PREP: 10 MIN. • **COOK:** 30 MIN.
MAKES: 6-8 SERVINGS

- **2 tablespoons butter**
- **1½ cups packed brown sugar**
- **1½ cups water**

DUMPLINGS

- **1¼ cups all-purpose flour**
- **½ cup sugar**
- **2 teaspoons baking powder**
- **½ teaspoon salt**
- **½ cup milk**
- **2 tablespoons butter, softened**
- **2 teaspoons vanilla extract**
- **½ cup coarsely chopped peeled apple, optional**

1. In a large skillet, heat the butter, brown sugar and water to boiling. Reduce heat to a simmer.

2. Meanwhile, in a large bowl, combine the dumplings ingredients. Drop by tablespoonfuls into the simmering sauce. Cover tightly and simmer 20 minutes. (Do not lift lid.) Serve warm with cream or ice cream if desired.

GRILLED CRANBERRY PEAR CRUMBLE

Fruit crisps are easy and quick to prepare, so I make them often! I created this fall-flavored grilled version with fresh pears and items I had on hand. My husband and I loved it.

—RONNA FARLEY ROCKVILLE, MD

START TO FINISH: 30 MIN.
MAKES: 6 SERVINGS

- 3 **medium ripe pears, sliced**
- ½ **cup dried cranberries**
- ¼ **cup sugar**
- 2 **tablespoons all-purpose flour**
- ¼ **teaspoon ground cinnamon**
- 1 **tablespoon butter**

TOPPING
- 2 **tablespoons butter, melted**
- ¼ **teaspoon ground cinnamon**
- 1 **cup granola without raisins**

1. Toss pears and cranberries with sugar, flour and cinnamon. Place 1 tablespoon butter in a 9-in. cast-iron skillet. Place on grill rack over medium heat until the butter is melted. Stir in fruit; grill, covered, until the pears are tender, 15-20 minutes, stirring occasionally.

2. For topping, mix the melted butter and cinnamon; toss with granola. Sprinkle over pears. Grill, covered, 5 minutes. Serve warm.

CARAMELIZED PINEAPPLE SUNDAES

Whenever we get a craving for a tropical escape, but can't actually leave town, this super-simple recipe does the trick! Drizzling the sauce over salted caramel ice cream and taking a bite is just plain paradise.

—ELISABETH LARSEN PLEASANT GROVE, UT

START TO FINISH: 30 MIN.
MAKES: 6 SERVINGS

- ¼ **cup butter, cubed**
- ½ **cup packed brown sugar**
- 1 **fresh pineapple, peeled and cut into ½-inch cubes**
- 3 **cups vanilla ice cream**
- ½ **cup flaked coconut, toasted**
- ½ **cup coarsely chopped macadamia nuts, toasted**

1. In a large skillet, heat butter over medium heat; stir in brown sugar. Add pineapple; cook and stir 8-10 minutes or until tender. Remove pineapple with a slotted spoon; set aside.

2. Bring the remaining juices to a simmer; cook for 3-4 minutes or until thickened. Remove from the heat. Layer the pineapple and ice cream into six dessert dishes; sprinkle with coconut and nuts. Drizzle with the sauce.

NOTE *To toast coconut, bake in a shallow pan in a 350° oven for 5-10 minutes or cook in a skillet over low heat until golden brown, stirring occasionally. To toast nuts, bake in a shallow pan in a 350° oven for 5-10 minutes or cook in a skillet over low heat until lightly browned, stirring occasionally.*

HELPFUL HINT

Shredded coconut keeps 4-6 months in the pantry and 6-8 months in the refrigerator. When it has gone bad, it will be brittle with a yellowish color.

MOM'S FRIED APPLES

PREP: 5 MIN. • **COOK:** 30 MIN.
MAKES: 6-8 SERVINGS

- ½ **cup butter, cubed**
- 6 **medium unpeeled tart red apples, sliced**
- ¾ **cup sugar, divided**
- ¾ **teaspoon ground cinnamon**

1. Melt butter in a large cast-iron or other ovenproof skillet. Add apples and ½ cup of the sugar; stir to mix well. Cover and cook over low heat for 20 minutes or until apples are tender, stirring frequently.

2. Add cinnamon and the remaining sugar. Cook and stir over medium-high heat 5-10 minutes longer.

Mom often made these rich, cinnamon-sugar apples when I was growing up. It's a trip down memory lane when I make them. The recipe is very dear to me.

—**MARGIE TAPPE** PRAGUE, OK

NOTES

INDEX